OLD-TIME BASEBALL

America's Pastime in the Gilded Age

HARVEY FROMMER

Guilford, Connecticut

An imprint of Rowman & Littlefield

Distributed by NATIONAL BOOK NETWORK

Copyright © 2017 by Harvey Frommer
First Taylor Trade hardback edition, 2006

British Library Cataloguing in Publication Information Available

Library of Congress Cataloging-in-Publication Data

The hardback edition of this book was previously cataloged by the Library of Congress as follows:

Frommer, Harvey.
  Old-time baseball : America's pastime in the gilded age / Harvey Frommer.
    p. cm.
  ISBN 1-58979-254-8 (cloth : alk. paper)
  1. Baseball—United States—History—19th century. I. Title.
GV863.A1F756 2006
  796.357'0973'09034—dc22

                                                              2005019236

ISBN 978-1-63076-006-9 (pbk.)
ISBN 978-1-63076-007-6 (e-book)

To the lovely Arielle Cecelia— "A.C."—
a book about the nineteenth century
for a child of the twenty-first

Base Ball

The Ball once struck off,
Away flies the Boy
To the next destin'd Post,
And the Home with Joy
—Anonymous, "A Little Pretty Pocket Book"

CONTENTS

Contents

ACKNOWLEDGMENTS

My wife Myrna always at the top of the list, always there for me as editor, confidante, and critic. The rest of the "home team": Jennifer and Jeff, Michele and Freddy, Laura and Ian.

Others who make the roster: Michael Aubrecht, Russ Cohen, Philip Speranza, Nick Anis, Patty Anis, Travis Nelson, Brad Horn of the National Baseball Hall of Fame at Cooperstown, Rick Rinehart, the hundreds on Frommersportslist, my friends at SABR. I thank you all.

Special thanks to my friends at the National Baseball Hall of Fame in Cooperstown, New York, for their kind permission granted to use material from Hall of Fame plaques in this book.

PREFACE

Even after ten years since this book's first publication in 2006, it remains one of my favorite works, delving deep into baseball's storied past, filled with all kinds of oddities and insights into the way things were when the world of sports was a far different place.

The early environment of baseball games was that of a gentlemen's affair marked by the absence of spectators, except for those invited by the teams. What spectators were there lolled about on the grass or sat on chairs and benches. The umpire was generally attired in tails and a tall black top hat, and in those early years he seated himself at a table along a baseline. Circa 1860, the general public became more and more involved as spectators, and winning replaced gentlemanly ways as baseball's operative factor.

The Cincinnati Red Stockings began playing in 1876 in the National League in a ball park located in an area known as Chester Park. In order to get to the ball game, fans had to ride on special trains or in carriages. Crowds of 3,000 were common and considered a good payday for the team. When the National League came into being, the White Stockings played their home games in a rickety wooden park on Dearborn between 23rd and 24th streets on Chicago's West Side.

During the 1880s and 1890s most parks were surrounded by wooden stands and a wooden fence. Some of the stands were partially protected by a roof, while others were simple wooden seats made of sun-bleached boards. That is how the word "bleachers" came to be. When those parks were filled to capacity, fans were allowed to stand around the infield or take up viewing perches in the far reaches of the outfield.

John B. Day transferred the Troy National League franchise to New York in 1883 and arrangements were made for games to be played on a polo field owned by James Gordon Bennett, publisher of the *New York Herald*. For most of the 1880s, the team played its games on a field at 110th Street and Fifth Avenue, across from Central Park's northeast corner. In 1897, a game between Boston and Baltimore drew more than 25,000 fans, the overflow crowd was permitted to stand just a few feet behind the infielders, creating a situation where any ball hit into the throng was ruled an automatic ground-rule double.

In 1899, the Giants moved to New York City plot 2106, lot 100, located between 155th and 157th streets at Eighth Avenue in upper Manhattan. The location was called "the new Polo Grounds," a horseshoe-shaped stadium with Coogan's Bluff on one side and the Harlem River on the other. The Polo Grounds seated 55,897, the most of any facility in the National League. A four-story, misshapen structure with seats close to the playing field and overhanging stands, it was an odd ball park that afforded fans the opportunity to be close to the action. There were 4,600 bleacher seats, 2,730 field boxes, 1,084 upper boxes, 5,138 upper reserved boxes, and 2,318 general admission seats. The majority of those who came to the Polo Grounds sat in the remaining lower general admission seats.

The visitors' bullpen was just a bench located in the boondocks of left center field. There was no shade from the sun for the visitors or protection from Giant fans who pelted opposing pitchers with pungent projectiles. The upper left field deck hung over the lower deck; and it was virtually impossible for a fly ball to get into the lower deck because of the projection of the upper deck. The overhang triggered many arguments, for if a ball happened to graze the front of the overhang it was a home run. The double decks in right field were even. The short distances and the asymmetrical shape of the convoluted ball park resulted in drives rebounding off the right field and left field walls like billiard shots. And over the years hitters and fielders on the New York Giants familiar with the pool table walls of the ball park had a huge advantage over opposing teams.

Fires and progress would make steel and concrete replace the wood and timber of the nineteenth century ball parks. The idiosyncratic dimensions of stadiums, the marching bands, even the real grass in many instances would ultimately become footnotes to baseball history.

As late as 1900 some clubs even allowed fans to park their automobiles or carriages in the outfield. The environment at those games made it difficult for fans to follow the action clearly. Even though scorecards and programs were sold, no public address system existed, and there were no names or numbers on the players' uniforms.

Players were sometimes pressed into service to double as ticket takers. And during breaks in the action on the field, the dull moments were enlivened by the festive performances of brass bands.

The St. Louis National League entry was known as the Browns and then the Perfectos—an odd name for a club with a not so perfect track record. The team left the National League twice, then returned and finished 12th twice, 11th three times, 10th once, 9th once, and once in 5th place in the years 1892–99.

To attract customers to Robinson Field, St. Louis owner Chris Von der Ahe transformed his ball park into what he called "the Coney Island of the West." He installed chute-the-chutes (tubs that plunged with their riders into a pool), night horseracing, and even a Wild West show. The popular tunes of the day were played by the Silver Cornet Band, an all-female aggregation bedecked in long striped skirts and elegant blouses with leg-of-mutton sleeves and broad white sailor hats.

In 1899 Chris Von der Ahe changed the uniforms around in his zest for more color. The new garments featured red trim and red-striped stockings. The new uniforms brought new nicknames for the St. Louis team—Cardinals or Redbirds, they were called, and so they would remain.

All of the above illustrates the curious and dramatic difference between the "then" and the "now" in the world of baseball. Just a taste of the fascinating content I collected to be a part of *Old-Time Baseball: America's Pastime in the Gilded Age.*

INTRODUCTION

I see great things in baseball; it's our game, the American game.
—Walt Whitman

This book is a trip back to another America in another century. Yet for me, it is bracketed by a different era: the time between 1975 when I wrote my first book, *A Baseball Century: The First Hundred Years of the National League,* and an evening in April 2005 at Yankee Stadium when the Yankees battled the Red Sox in the initial series that year between the age-old rivals.

In 1975, my appreciation of the game of baseball deepened and expanded from the wonderful and rare privilege I had of flying across the United States with the Philadelphia Phillies and going from ballpark to ballpark interviewing players and other baseball personnel. Those full days and nights spread over much of the summer of that year made me acutely aware of the hold of the game on America, of its roots, its idiosyncrasies, its magic. The experience confirmed my sense that writing about sports was something I really wanted to do.

The Yankee Stadium experience, on the other hand, gave me pause. Baseball in 2005, especially in that huge ballpark in the Bronx and involving the Yankees–Red Sox rivalry, which I have written and spoken about in depth, was many years away from baseball in 1975 and more than a century away from the "Old-Time Baseball" that is the subject of this book.

"Let us go forth awhile, and get better air in our lungs. Let us leave our closed rooms . . . the game of ball is glorious."
—Walt Whitman

The blaring rock music, the private boxes filled with people who too often have scant knowledge of and even less feeling for the game, the extravagant prices for food, souvenirs, programs reveal a sport that has exploded into crass commercialism fueled by print and electronic media providing more facts and factoids than anyone could reasonably need or deserve.

In 2005, 390 major leaguers earned a million dollars or more for the season. The average opening-day salary was a record $2.6 million. The payroll of the New York Yankees was a tad below $200 million, more than the combined payrolls of the bottom five teams.

And the Boston Red Sox, second to the Yankees were, with a payroll of $121.3 million, not too far behind. No one could have imagined what the game would become in the middle of the first decade of the 21st century back in the 19th century when it all began.

"Old-time baseball," was a time of amateurs in pre–Civil War America, of Abner Doubleday, Alexander Cartwright and the Knickerbocker Club, the National Association of Base Ball Players, Harry Wright and the Cincinnati Red Stockings—the first real "professionals," the National League of Professional Baseball Clubs, rivals like the American Association, the Union Association, the Players League . . .

All that is in place now was seeded in that earlier game—the box score, earned run averages, free agency, the reserve clause, unions, records, stats, organizations, spring training, postseason play, stars, big business, media's nonblinking eye.

> "The game of baseball has now become beyond question the leading feature of the outdoor sports of the United States. . . . It is a game which is peculiarly suited to the American temperament and disposition; . . . in short, the pastime suits the people, and the people suit the pastime."
>
> —Charles A. Peverelly, 1866

It is fashionable, some might say mandatory, to delve deeply into the origins of baseball. The debunking of the Cooperstown myth notwithstanding, there are those who go a step further and question whether Alexander Cartwright did in fact set down the parameters of the game as we know it today and in doing so become the Father of the Game. Yet, even Cartwright's plaque at the National Baseball Hall of Fame at Cooperstown refers to him as the "Father of Modern Baseball."

Baseball's origin detectives/archaeologists have come up with a range of flashes over recent years: 1344, a group of monks and nuns in a French manuscript are shown playing a game with a strong resemblance to coed softball; 1791, the first known record in America of the term "baseball" traced to Pittsfield, Massachusetts; 1744, an English children's book made what some construe to be a reference to the game; 1937, an Italian demographer came upon blonde-haired Berber tribesmen in the desert in Libya playing a game that resembled baseball . . .

It would seem, with apologies to Robert Frost, these theorists are claiming the game was ours before we were the game's.

Still old-time baseball exerts a pull, a fascination. Figures from that long ago time peer out of faded photographs, some with mustaches, others with beards, others with the clean-shaven faces of innocents playing ball in a less sophisticated time. They were the pioneers, the trailblazers.

By the end of the 19th century, baseball was a sport that provided a step up, a glamorous career opportunity for youth coming out of lower socioeconomic origins. Few of them ever attended college. For the most part, their playing careers were short, and afterwards they moved into blue-collar jobs.

Many of the players came from big cities, especially the booming northeastern metropolitan areas. In 1897, for example, just three out of 168 National League players came from as far south as Virginia. Only seven players came from the west, while more than a third of the athletes were born in Pennsylvania or Massachusetts.

All of them were white (with a couple of short-lived exceptions), most were of German or Irish backgrounds. Fun-loving, generous spenders, the 19th-century baseball players were a lively assortment of athletes who brought a verve, a daring, a love to the game that enabled the sport to surmount obstacles and to prevail.

So come, let us celebrate old-time baseball.

ONE

The March of Baseball Time

Baseball is the very symbol, the outward and visible expression of the drive and push and rush and struggle of the raging, tearing, booming nineteenth century.
—*Mark Twain*

1834

The first book of instructions for baseball appeared: *The Book of Sports.*

1845

September 23: The Knickerbocker Baseball Club of New York was organized at the suggestion of Alexander J. Cartwright, who created rules to distinguish his brand of baseball from other forms played throughout the country.

1846

June 19: The first recorded baseball game took place. Alexander Cartwright's Knickerbockers lost to the New York Baseball Club at the Elysian Fields, in Hoboken, New Jersey. The New York Club defeated the Knickerbockers 23–1.

1849

The Knickerbockers were the first team to wear an official uniform.

1851

June 3: The Knickerbockers won their first match of the year, 21–11, against the Washington Club. According to Cartwright's rules, the first team scoring 21 runs won the game.

1856

September 15: The first reported game of baseball in Canada was played in London, Ontario. The London Club defeated the Delaware club 34–33.

December 5: Baseball was first dubbed the "National Pastime" by the *New York Mercury*.

1857

January 22: The first baseball convention was staged in New York. Called by the Knickerbockers, it was attended by 16 baseball clubs, all located on Manhattan and Long Island. The nine-inning game was adopted, bypassing the old rules of the first team scoring 21 runs winning.

March 7: The rules committee stated that nine innings should constitute an official game rather than a team scoring nine runs. For the first time, rules mandated nine men to a side, even though the game had been played that way since 1845.

March 10: The National Association of Base Ball Players (NABBP), the first league in baseball, was formed.

May 13: Attended by representatives of 10 New England baseball clubs, a convention was held in Dedham, Massachusetts. Playing rules under the name of "Massachusetts Association of Base Ball Players" were to contrast the differences with the "New York Game."

October 22: In an all-Brooklyn match, the Atlantic Club defeated the Eckford Club taking the best-of-three-games match, claiming the championship for 1857. The baseball custom then was that the championship was only won by the team who defeated the current titleholder two out of three games.

1858

July 20: Paying fifty cents, some 1,500 fans attended an All-Star Game at the Fashion Race Course on Long Island.

1859

November 28: The first baseball club on the West Coast was organized, the Eagle Club of San Francisco.

1860

March 14: The Nassau Base Ball Club was organized on the Princeton campus.

March 15: The annual meeting of the National Association of Base Ball Players was held. Rule 36 was amended: "No party shall be competent to play in a match who receives compensation for his services."

July 1: At Pittsfield, Massachusetts, Amherst and Williams colleges played their first intercollegiate baseball match. Amherst won,

73–32. The game was played under the rules of the "Massachusetts Game."

1861

October 21: The Grand Match for the Silver Ball was played on the Mutuals' Grounds at Hoboken. All-star teams from Brooklyn and New York competed. Star hurler Jim Creighton pitched his Brooklyn team to an 18–6 triumph over New York before 15,000. The Silver Ball Trophy, the same size as a regular baseball, was kept by Brooklyn, the club whose members scored the most runs during the match.

1862

May 15: The Union Baseball Grounds at Marcy Avenue and Rutledge Street in Brooklyn was opened. It was the first enclosed ball field to charge an admission fee.

December 25: More than 40,000 watched two teams of Union soldiers compete in a baseball game at Hilton Head, South Carolina.

1865

August 30: President Andrew Johnson brought the first organized baseball team (referred to as "a delegation of the National Base Ball Club") to the White House/Presidential Mansion for a visit.

1866

December 12: The 10th annual convention of the NABBP was staged. A record 202 clubs sent delegates.

1867

December 9: The NABBP banned blacks participating in the league "on political grounds."

1868

April 25: The *New York Clipper* announced that it would award a gold ball of regulation weight and size to the club dubbed champions of 1868. In addition, gold medals would also be given to the nine best players.

August 4: A 50-minute game—the fastest on record—was played in Brooklyn at the Union Grounds. Al Martin held the Uniques to one run against the Eckfords' 37.

1869

May 4: The Cincinnati Red Stockings, baseball's first admittedly all-professional team, played their first game of the year. They trounced the Great Westerns 45–9.

June 26: President Ulysses S. Grant hosted the Cincinnati Red Stockings at the White House.

September 18: The Pythians defeated the City Items, 27–17. It marked the first time an all-black team played an exhibition game against an all-white team.

1870

June 14: After 84 straight wins, the Cincinnati Red Stockings were defeated, 8–7, by the Atlantics of Brooklyn.

July 3: The Knickerbockers withdrew formally from the NABBP, protesting the trend toward professionalism.

November 10: At the New York State Base Ball Convention in Albany, a motion passed that no club in New York composed of colored men would be admitted to the National Association.

1871

March 17: The first professional baseball league, the National Association of Professional Base Ball Players, was founded in New York City. The organization's charter members included the Cincinnati Red Stockings, Chicago White Stockings, Cleveland Forest Citys, Fort Wayne Kekiongas, New York Mutuals, Philadelphia Athletics, Rockford Forest Citys, Troy Haymakers, and Washington Olympics.
May 4: The National Association played its first game. Forest City defeated Fort Wayne 2–0.
May 16: Boston's first professional game was played. The Troy Haymakers defeated the Red Stockings, 29–14.
The first batting averages were recorded, starting with Boston and Cleveland.

1872

April 13: An auction of memorabilia from the 1869 tour of the Red Stockings was held at Union Grounds in Cincinnati. People paid two to four dollars for baseballs.

1873

July 30: After a three-week holiday spent in Cape May—claimed as needed rest from the exhaustion of the season—the Philadelphia Athletics were defeated in Boston, 24–10.

1874

January 29: Albert Spalding arrived in England to push his plan on sports editors and athletes to bring two baseball teams over in the summer to show off American baseball and get in some cricket matches.

1875

September 11: The first baseball game with women professionals was played in Springfield, Illinois, on a half-sized diamond with a nine-foot-high canvas surrounding the field. Uniforms were similar to those worn by males except that the pants were shorter. The final score was "Blondes" 42, "Brunettes" 38.

1876

The National League of Professional Baseball was formed with eight teams: Boston Red Caps, Chicago White Stockings, Cincinnati Reds, Hartford Dark Blues, Louisville Grays, Philadelphia Athletics, Brooklyn Mutuals, and St. Louis Brown Stockings. All owners agreed to play a 70-game schedule between April 22 and October 21.

April 22: The first National League game was played. The Red Stockings defeated the Athletics, 6–5. Davy Force was credited with the first assist. Jim O'Rourke got the first hit and first single. Tim McGinley was credited with the first run scored. Levi Meyerle slugged the first double.

April 24: Levi Meyerle was credited with the first triple.

May 2: Ross Barnes recorded the first home run.

May 6: Bill Harbidge, playing for Hartford, was the first left-handed catcher.

May 25: The Philadelphia Athletics and Louisville Grays played to a 2–2 tie, the first in major league history.

June 14: George Hall, Philadelphia Athletics, became the first player ever to hit for the cycle.

July 15: George Bradley recorded the first no-hitter in National League history

September 19: Candy Cummings was the first to pitch and win two complete games in one day.

October 23: The *Chicago Tribune* published a new statistic, dividing at-bats by hits—"batting percentage" was the new term used.

1877

The first rule appeared stating the ball must stay in fair territory to be a hit.

The first printed schedule appeared.

Syracuse Stars catcher Pete Hotaling became the first professional catcher to wear a mask. Harvard captain Fred Thayer originally designed the device to protect his teammate Jim Tyng.

March 5: Hartford finalized arrangements for its home games to be played in Brooklyn at the Union Grounds but retained its identity as the Hartford Dark Blues.

July 13: Chicago's George Bradley received the day off. He had pitched the previous 89 consecutive games.

1878

February 12: Frederick Winthrop Thayer of Massachusetts received a patent for baseball's first catcher's mask.

May 8: Paul Hines was credited as the first player to turn an unassisted triple play.

July 15: John Ward, 18, made his first major league start. He lost 13–9, but continued to pitch for Providence every inning of every game for the rest of the season.

December 31: A report was circulated that 8,000,000 bats had been sold in the United States in 1878.

1879

March 25: The National League voted to keep the 50-cent admission price to all baseball games.

April 4: Providence created a centerfield "bull pen" in the Messer Street Grounds. Fans who arrived after the fifth inning paid but 15 cents. The Grays built the first safety net behind the catcher to protect the fans.

1880

February 12: Boston reduced its season ticket prices from $14 to $12 as a result of the Red Stockings failure to record their third straight championship.

April 14: The new Cincinnati ballpark on Bank Street was inaugurated with an exhibition game between the Reds and the Washington Nationals. Seating 3,490, the park served pro teams in three leagues: National League in 1880, American Association in 1882–1883, and Union Association in 1884.

May 20: The first "pitching rotation" was created when Cap Anson alternated Larry Corcoran and Fred Goldsmith.

June 10: Charley Jones of the Boston Red Caps was the first player to hit two home runs in a single game.

June 12: John Lee Richmond of the Worcester Ruby Legs pitched the first perfect game in major league history, nipping the visiting Cleveland Blues 1–0.

October: The National League outlawed Sunday baseball and banned the sale of beer at all games. Cincinnati refused to comply and was expelled from the league by NL president William Hulbert.

1881

The National League adopted an 84-game schedule.

The owners voted to stop giving refunds or rain checks for postponed games.

August 21: In a game in Louisville, the Eclipses banned black catcher Moses Fleetwood Walker from playing with the visiting Cleveland Blues.

September 10: With two outs in the bottom of the ninth and his team trailing by three runs, Roger Connor won the game by hitting the first grand slam in big league history.

September 27: A dozen fans stayed through a rainstorm to watch their hometown hero Chicago White Stockings defeat the Troy Trojans 10–8. It was the smallest paying crowd in major league history.

November 2: "Liberty for all" was the motto of the new rival major league—the American Association of Professionals, formed in St. Louis to compete against the Nationals.

1882

For the first time, teams in the National League were permitted to wear colored uniforms.

Paul Hines was the first player to wear sunglasses on the field.

Pete Browning was the first player to have his bats custom made.

March 15: Providence raised the price of season tickets from $15 to $20.

July 18: Ambidextrous Tony Mullane of the Louisville Eclipse pitched right- and left-handed during a 9–8 loss to the Baltimore Orioles.

September 25: The Brown Stockings charged fans one admission price but permitted them to see both ends of a doubleheader. Prior to this fans were charged two separate admissions.

December: The American Association became the first league to hire full-time umpires.

1883

January 13: New York's American Association and National League teams made news. They announced that they would play at the

Polo Grounds on separate diamonds. An eight-foot fence would separate the action.

During the preseason, the American Association and National League agreed to terms of peace, including a promise not to raid players from each other's league.

March 14: In a Northwestern League meeting, Peoria attempted to ban blacks to prevent Toledo from playing star C. Moses Fleetwood Walker. After what was termed an "exciting discussion," the motion was withdrawn. Walker was allowed to play.

September 13: Cleveland's Hugh Daily, a one-armed pitcher, hurled a 1–0 no-hitter against Philadelphia. Known as "One Arm," Daily pitched six seasons in the major leagues, compiling a 73–87 record.

The American Association champion Philadelphia Athletics lost their first eight postseason exhibition games, resulting in the cancellation of a "World Series" against the NL pennant-winning Boston Beaneaters.

1884

The National League schedule was expanded to 112 games.

April 18: The New York Giants and Brooklyn Trolley-Dodgers met for the first time in a major league ball game.

May 1: Moses Fleetwood Walker became the first black player to appear in a major league game. He went hitless in three at-bats with Toledo of the American Association, a major league at the time.

Bud Hillerich created his first custom wooden bat for Pete Browning, a Louisville player. The Louisville Slugger was in baseball to stay.

The first postseason games were played—National League versus the American Association.

Union Association outfielder Harry Wheeler became the only player ever to appear with five separate teams during the same season: five games with the St. Louis Browns (in the AA), Union Association's Kansas City Unions (20 games), Chicago Browns (17), Pittsburgh Stoogies (17), and Baltimore Monumentals (17).

Philadelphia Keystones catcher Jack Clements became the first player ever to wear a chest protector in a major league game. Roger Bresnahan later popularized the device.

1885

Spring Training got under way as Cap Anson and his Chicago White Stockings traveled to Hot Springs, Arkansas, to prepare for the upcoming season.

Art Irwin of the Providence Grays developed the first known fielder's glove after padding a buckskin glove to protect his two broken fingers.

American Association St. Louis Browns and National League champion Chicago White Stockings went head-to-head in six championship games (winning three each), resulting in a rare tie. Despite the forming of a special committee to determine a winner, both teams were declared champions and split the $1,000 purse—$500 each.

March 15: A New York lower court ruled that playing baseball on Sunday was a crime. This decision was overturned, but it was then appealed.

September 10: Joe Harrington became the first player to hit a home run in his first at-bat.

October 1: The Cuban Giants were organized and became the first team of professional black players.

October 22: The Brotherhood of Professional Base Ball Players was formed by John M. Ward and a few teammates.

1886

March 17: The first issue of the *Sporting News* was published.

April 22: The modern new park of the Mets opened on Staten Island. Later in the season fans watched from the St. George grandstand as the Statue of Liberty was being put together.

June 16: The Southern League of Colored Base Ballists became the first black sports league. Their first game was played on this date. The league disbanded in August.

Guy Hecker of the American Association Louisville Colonels became the first player to lead a league in both hitting and pitching, with 52 wins and a .341 average.

1887

February 14: Mike "King" Kelly was sold by the White Sox for $10,000 to the Red Sox.

The National League St. Louis Maroons was sold to a group from Indianapolis for $12,000, including players. The Maroons became the Hoosiers.

March 14: In Baltimore, the National Colored League was organized. Charter members were Lord Baltimore, Pythians (Philadelphia), Keystones (Pittsburgh), Gorhams (New York), Falls City (Louisville), and Resolutes (Boston).

April 16: Mike Griffin of the Baltimore Orioles became the first player ever to homer in his first major league at-bat.

May 6: The National Colored League played its inaugural game, as the Gorhams defeated the Keystones, 11–8. Ten days later the league disbanded.

The Philadelphia Quakers finished off their 1887 season with an unprecedented 16 consecutive wins.

Detroit Wolverines owner Frederick Stearnes challenged American Association St. Louis owner Chris Von der Ahe to a best-of-15 championship series. The Wolverines prevailed, winning eight games. Despite appearing in 16 postseason games, the Browns received nothing for their efforts, as Von der Ahe refused to share his profits.

American Association Philadelphia Athletics pitcher Fred Chapman became the youngest player ever to take the mound in the major leagues. He pitched five innings against the Cleveland Spiders. He was 14 years old.

St. Louis Browns first-baseman/manager Charles Comiskey became the first baseball player ever paid to endorse a product after lending his name and likeness to Menell's Penetrating Oil.

The first rule defining the strike zone appeared.

November 17: The National League officially recognized the Brotherhood by meeting with a committee of three players, John Ward, Ned Hanlon, and Dan Brouthers.

1888

February 23: James "Pud" Galvin signed with Pittsburgh for $3,000, including $1,000 in advance. He had been offered $3,500 with no advance money, but Galvin needed the $1,000 to get him through the winter.

March 20: Albert Spalding announced that his Chicago team and a squad of National League All-Stars would go on a baseball tour to Australia the following winter.

April 18: American Association umpire John Gaffney became the first to move behind the pitcher with men on base.

Cincinnati Red Stockings fans were able to follow the game using the first-ever baseball scorecard.

"Casey at the Bat" was published in the *San Francisco Examiner.* Ernest L. Thayer, 25, was paid $5 for his efforts and was simply credited as "Phin."

The National League champion New York Giants defeated the American Association's St. Louis Browns (four-time AA pennant winners) in an eight-game championship series. St. Louis owner Chris Von der Ahe kept the Browns' $1,200 pennant purse while referring to his players as "chumps." His team had now played in 27 postseason games (over two seasons) without being paid.

1889

January 1: The Around-the-World touring squads played a New Year's game in Melbourne, Australia. The Chicagos nipped the All-Americas 9–8.

February 9: All-America defeated Chicago 10–6 in the shadow of the pyramids outside of Cairo. Manager Cap Anson apologized to the Sphinx for his team's poor play.

March 20: A Mr. Hiroka of Tokyo sent a letter to a New York sporting goods house ordering bats, balls, and other baseball equipment. The letter explained that baseball "has been played there for several months" and that a baseball association was in the process of formation.

March 22: The All-America team edged Chicago 7–6 in England's Old Trafford Cricket Stadium. The *Manchester Guardian* reported the "general verdict of the more than 1,000 spectators was that the American game was 'slow' and 'wanting' in variety."

August 10: New York's Mickey Welch became the first pinch hitter in major league history. He struck out.

October 6: The Brooklyn Dodgers established a major league record for attendance: 353,690 for 70 dates.

December 16: The Players League was formed.

1890

March 27: The Inter-State League application of an all-black club made up of former Cuban Giants was rejected.

New York Giants slugger Mike Tiernan became the first player ever to hit a home run from one ballpark into another after launching a 13th-inning blast off the Boston Beaneaters' "Kid" Nichols that traveled over the center field wall at the Polo Grounds into the adjacent Brotherhood Park.

Brooklyn Bridegrooms and Cincinnati Reds moved from the American Association to the National League, which had also dropped the Washington Senators. The AA's Kansas City franchise folded, but the Rochester Hop Bitters, Syracuse Stars, Toledo Maumees, and Brooklyn Gladiators were added in their place.

The newly developed Players League debuted with eight teams: Boston, Brooklyn, Buffalo, Chicago, Cleveland, New York, Philadelphia, and Pittsburgh. The Buffalo Bisons recorded the greatest opening-day winning margin with a 23–2 victory over the Cleveland Infants.

On Labor Day, the Pittsburgh Alleghenys were swept in a rare triple-header by the home team Brooklyn Bridegrooms 10–9, 3–2, and 8–4.

The short-lived Players League folded in December, returning all of their players to their original teams. The Pittsburgh franchise deviated from the agreement, though, and signed second baseman Louis Bierbauer, who had originally belonged to the Philadelphia Phillies. After being accused in the papers of being "Pirates," the team adopted the nickname and refused to return Bierbauer to their cross-state rivals.

1891

February 17: The American Association met and unseated President Thurman, then withdrew from the National Agreement. The AA's first move was to switch its franchise from Chicago to Cincinnati to compete with the National League in the Queen City.

April 27: The Bridegrooms played their home opener in the East New York section of Brooklyn in Eastern Park, which was a Players League facility the year before. The ballpark was situated near a hub of streetcar lines creating a situation where fans dodged trolleys. "Trolley-Dodgers," later shortened to "Dodgers," became the name for the team as a result.

May 1: Cleveland opened new League Park at 66th and Lexington before 9,500. Cy Young pitched the Spiders to a 12–3 victory over the Reds.

July 31: Amos Rusie of the New York Giants, 20, became the youngest pitcher ever to hurl a no-hitter. He shut out the Brooklyn Trolley-Dodgers 6–0.

August 26: Shortstop John J. McGraw debuted for the American Association Baltimore Orioles. The "Blackbirds" nipped the Columbus Buckeyes, 6–5.

September 4: "Old Man" Cap Anson appeared wearing a wig and a long white beard before a delighted Chicago crowd. Anson wore this costume throughout the game. His Colts trounced the Beaneaters, 5–3.

The Boston Beaneaters won the National League Pennant, while the cross-town rival Reds took the American Association title. For undisclosed reasons, the NL champs declined an invitation for a playoff, resulting in no baseball championship for the first time since 1883.

October 4: Ted Breitenstein of the St. Louis Browns became the first pitcher ever to debut with a no-hitter. He shut out the Louisville Colonels, 8–0.

The American Association ceased operation in December, leaving the Baltimore Orioles, St. Louis Browns, Louisville Colonels, and Washington Senators to be absorbed into the National League the following season.

1892

January 9: "Slide, Kelly, Slide," by George Gaskin, made the popular music charts, the first baseball song to do so.

April 17: The first Sunday game was played in the National League. Cincinnati defeated St. Louis, 5–1.

April 30: Dr. S. B. Talcott, superintendent of the State Lunatic Asylum in New York, was quoted in the *New York Clipper*: "I believe that baseball is a homeopathic cure for lunacy. It is a kind of craze in itself, and gives the lunatics a new kind of crazing to relieve them of the malady which afflicts their minds."

May 14: Tom Daly, playing for Brooklyn, became the first pinch hitter in major league history to get a hit—he homered.

June 6: President Benjamin Harrison watched as Washington was defeated 7–4 by Cincinnati in 11 innings. It was the first visit to a major league game by a United States president. On June 25, Harrison attended his second game, becoming the first to attend two major league baseball games while in office.

The Boston Beaneaters defeated the Cleveland Spiders for the World Championship title. Team president Arthur Soden divided the $1,000 purse between his 13 players, with each receiving $76.92 (or $12.82 per game).

1893

February 4: The first recorded version of "Casey at the Bat," sung by Russell Hunting, made the music charts. DeWolf Hopper's more famous version would not be released until October 1906.

March 7: The National League eliminated the pitching box and added a pitcher's rubber five feet behind the previous back line of the box, establishing the modern pitching distance of 60 feet 6 inches (the extra six inches were as a result of an error on the handwritten instructions). A distance of 93 feet between the bases was also proposed along with a 12 × 4 inch slab of rubber to replace the pitcher's box.

Bats flattened on one side to facilitate bunting were banned.

The National League owners established a new postseason best-of-seven playoff series known as the Temple Cup (named after Pittsburgh Pirates president Chase Temple). The winning team would be awarded a two-foot-tall silver cup valued at $800 after winning the series a minimum of three times.

August 16: Baltimore's Bill Hawk became the first pitcher ever to record a no-hitter from the new 60-foot, 6-inch mound distance. It was a win over the Washington Senators. Wilbert Robinson was the catcher.

1894

February 26: Rules changes went into effect to help pitchers. Foul bunts would now be called strikes. The infield fly rule was instituted.

March 12: Free season tickets for ladies for Tuesday and Friday games were issued by Pittsburgh.

May 30: Boston Beaneater Bob Lowe became the first player ever to hit four home runs in a game. All four were hit over the wall off Cincinnati's Elton Chamberlain in a 20–11 win.

June 16: Ed Delahanty went six-for-six with a double, as Philadelphia ripped Cincinnati 19–9.

June 30: Fred Clarke went five-for-five in his first major league game and set a record, but his Louisville club lost 13–6 to Philadelphia.

The Philadelphia Phillies outfield finished the season with a cumulative .400 batting average—the best ever from a single team. Sam Thompson hit .404, Ed Delahanty .400, and Billy Hamilton .399. The next-best outfield came from the Detroit Tigers in 1925 who combined for a .380 average.

1895

April 12: Cincinnati defeated the Page Fence Giants for the second straight day. It was a rare matchup between a major league team and a black team.

May 6: The Philadelphia–Louisville game was postponed due to the running of the Kentucky Derby.

May 23: The Louisville Colonels lost to Brooklyn because they ran out of baseballs. Responsibility for supplying baseballs rested with the home team, Louisville, who began the game with just three baseballs, including two practice balls borrowed from Brooklyn. By the third inning, the balls were worn out and not usable. The messenger sent to get new ones never returned. Louisville was forced to forfeit the game.

June 15: Future novelist Zane Grey made his minor league debut in left field for Findlay, Ohio, against Wheeling in the Tri-State League. The Pennsylvania University athlete went hitless.

August 3: The Capital Colored All-Americans sailed for England with a squad of players from Western League clubs.

August 12: Heavyweight boxing champion Jim Corbett played first base for Scranton as they defeated Buffalo in an Eastern League game. The champ had two singles and drove in two runs.

1896

July 12: Ed Delahanty of the Philadelphia Phillies hit four inside-the-park homers (for seven RBIs) off Bill Terry of the Chicago Colts.

October 4: The Cuban Giants defeated the Chicago Unions 11–9 to claim the title of black champions of America.

The Baltimore Orioles (90–29), winners of three consecutive pennants, met the second-place Cleveland Spiders (80–48) for a classic rematch of the Temple Cup. The defending champion Spiders were swept in the playoffs.

December: Princeton University's Professor Charles E. Hinton introduced baseball's first automated pitching machine.

1897

April 19: The Washington Senators were welcomed in the Oval Office by President William McKinley.

April 22: Wee Willie Keeler slapped a single and double in what was game 1 of his 44-game batting streak.

May 16: Fans assembled for Cleveland's first Sunday baseball game only to watch as police arrested players after the first inning. Bail was provided by Cleveland club owner Frank DeHaas Robison and players and umpire Tim Hurst were released. A test case was made of rookie hurler John Powell. On June 10, he was found guilty of playing ball on Sunday and fined $5.

July 18: Cap Anson became the first player to achieve 3,000 hits. His total was changed to 2,995, then restored more than a century later.

December 31: Charles Hercules Ebbets, who began with the organization as a ticket taker, gained 10 percent interest in the Brooklyn National League team and the title of president.

1898

The first modern rules defining a balk and stolen base appeared.
The first official recording of base stealing statistics appeared.
June 13: Former hurler Charles Sweeney, late of the San Quentin penitentiary where he had served time for manslaughter, umpired the San Francisco–San Jose game in the California League.
July 5: Lizzie Arlington became the first woman ever to play in an organized baseball game after pitching a single inning for Reading in the Eastern League. Atlantic League president Ed Barrow later hired her to participate in exhibition games around the country.

1899

February 25: The National League Committee on Rules recommended that authority be given to umpires to fine unruly players $10 for a first offense.
May 15: Willie Keeler, one of the smallest players in baseball, slammed the ball to left field past startled Ed Delahanty of the Phillies. Keeler had an inside-the-park grand slam in Brooklyn's 8–5 victory.
October 8: Three teams played in a single doubleheader at Chicago. Game 1 pitted the hometown Orphans against the Cleveland Spiders, as Jake Taylor tossed his first shutout and 39th complete game of the season en route to a 13–0 Chicago victory. Game 2 matched the winners against the Louisville Colonels and ended with another 7–3 Chicago decision, after the game was called because of darkness after only five innings.

1900

February 8: In New York City, workers were dismantling fences at the Polo Grounds to cut a street through the property, leaving the Giants without a home for the coming season.

February 19: The tour staged its first game in Europe, playing in Naples, Italy.

February 22: At the Villa Borghese outside of Rome, the Chicagos edged the All-Americas 3–2 before a crowd that included King Humbert of Italy.

February 25: The Tourists played their final game in Italy, with the All-Americas winning 7–4 in Florence.

February 28: John McGraw and Wilbert Robinson both signed contracts with Baltimore. When the team disbanded, both refused to report to Brooklyn. They sat out the first third of the season and were finally traded to St. Louis.

April 13: Umpire Tim Hurst, at the urging of Cincinnati and New York owners, was banned from working in cities where club owners "object to having a man of that type associated with their grounds, where ladies and gentlemen watch the games." Hurst had a reputation as a colorful, controversial character.

March 8: At the Fifth Avenue Hotel in New York, the National League met and voted to go with eight teams. Baltimore owners were paid off $30,000 for their franchise; Charles Ebbets and Ned Hanlon reserved the right to sell the players. Cleveland, Louisville, and Washington received $10,000 each. Louisville owner Barney Dreyfuss sent most of his players to his Pittsburgh team.

1953

June 3: Congress cited New York City librarian Robert Henderson's research and book *Bat, Ball and Bishop* in proving that Alexander Cartwright "founded" baseball and not Abner Doubleday.

1956

January 19: The City of Hoboken dedicated a plaque to honor the achievements of Alexander Cartwright in organizing early baseball at Elysian Field in New Jersey.

TWO

Roots

Baseball has the great advantage over cricket of being ended sooner. . . .
It combines the best features of the primitive form of cricket known as
Tip and Run, with those of lawn tennis, Puss-in-the-Corner,
and Handel's Messiah.
—George Bernard Shaw

THE INVENTION OF BASEBALL

Mythology coats baseball history; some would say mythology lacquers baseball history. And although the myth has been repeatedly denigrated that Abner Doubleday was the inventor of the sport, he still is acknowledged in many quarters as the father of the national pastime.

The story claims "base ball" was first played in 1839, in Cooperstown, New York, between the boys of Otsego Academy and a team from Green's Select School. That game, "town ball," had such loose rules that all hits were fair and boys with impunity could run headlong into each other. Abner Doubleday, as the story goes, a young Otsego player, reportedly sat down right there on the spot and created the rules that led to the game of baseball.

```
┌─────────────────────────────────────────┐
│  ┌───────────────────────────────────┐  │
│  │                                   │  │
│  │          DOUBLEDAY FIELD          │  │
│  │   WHERE BASEBALL WAS INVENTED     │  │
│  │   AND FIRST PLAYED IN 1839        │  │
│  │                                   │  │
│  └───────────────────────────────────┘  │
└─────────────────────────────────────────┘
```

—Sign put up by the New York Highway Department,
a longtime feature of Cooperstown, New York

The game's actual parent was Alexander Joy Cartwright, Jr., a descendant of British sea captains. In 1842 Cartwright, then 22 years old, was part of a group of young men from New York City's financial district who enjoyed playing "base ball" on a vacant lot on 27th Street and Fourth Avenue in Manhattan. Three years later, the group, numbering 28 men, the "yuppies of their time," prosperous, middle-class types, organized themselves into the Knickerbockers Baseball Club, with a restricted membership of 40 males and annual dues of five dollars. The name was derived from the Knickerbocker Engine Company, where Cartwright had cheerfully served for a time as a volunteer fireman.

As Manhattan continued to grow and suitable space became less and less available for the playing of the game of base ball, the Knickerbockers began taking the ferry across the Hudson River to Hoboken, New Jersey. They played on weekends and practiced twice a week on an ancient cricket playground. Their new grounds, Elysian Fields, was conveniently lined not only with trees but taverns as well. It was a peaceful meadow nestled beside the banks of the Hudson River.

The following year, it was the 25-year-old Cartwright (aided by Daniel Lucas "Doc" Adams, a physician from New Hampshire) who created a new set of rules and regulations transforming baseball forever. The infield would be diamond-shaped, 90 feet to a side, with a base at each corner. There would be foul lines, nine players a side, and nine innings to a game. Punctuality for the players was mandated. The new rules also specified three outs allowed per side per inning. First and third bases were located 42 paces apart. Pitchers had to throw the ball underhanded, keeping the wrist and elbow straight.

An umpire along the third base line would sit at a table; there were times he would be dressed in tails and a tall black hat. No strikes or balls were called. The batter was allowed three missed swings before he was out. When disputes arose, the umpire was solicited for his opinion. He also had the option of getting feedback from spectators before ruling on fly balls. Most important, the runner was to be tagged or thrown out, not thrown at.

"Soaking" or "plugging"—firing the ball at a runner to retire him, a painful practice—was eliminated. The rules stated: "A player running the bases shall be out if the ball is in the hands of an adversary on the base, or the runner is touched with it before he makes his bases; it being understood, however, that in no instance however is a ball to be thrown at him." Cartwright's rules also specified that a game ended when a team scored 21 "aces" or runs. And fielders produced outs by catching a batted ball on the first bounce, catching a ball on the fly in the air, tossing the ball to a base ahead of the runner, or tagging a runner out between bases.

"Let him hit it—you've got fielders behind you."
—Alexander Cartwright, 1846

With the new set of rules for the new game in place, the Knickerbockers, now bedecked in white flannel shirts, blue woolen pantaloons, and spiffy straw hats, advertised a challenge match to any team willing to test their mettle.

On June 19, 1846, the first officially recorded baseball game was played at the Elysian Fields between the Knickerbockers and the New York Nine. Cartwright umpired the contest, enforcing a six-cent fine, payable on the spot, for swearing. The Knickerbockers were routed 23–1 by the New York Nine. And the first baseball game was in the record books.

Although Alexander Joy Cartwright was the "father" of American baseball, he did not stay around long enough to see the growth of his child. On March 1, 1849, he left New York City (his bat, ball, and rule book with him) and made the long trip to California—one of hundreds of thousands lured by the discovery of gold, prodded by the dream of getting rich quick.

His diary notation of April 23, 1849, written in Independence, Missouri, a stopover on his way west, related:

> During the past week we have passed the time in fixing wagon-covers, stowing property, etc., varied by hunting and fishing and playing base ball. It is comical to see the mountain men and Indians playing the new game. I have the ball with me that we used back home [New York].

Cartwright did not tarry long in California, for he was put off by the frenzy and fervor of those questing for gold. He moved on to Hawaii, becoming one of Honolulu's leading merchants and bankers, founding its library and fire department. He was fire chief for a decade. The energetic Cartwright also managed the finances of Hawaii's royal family. In his spare time he also promoted baseball. He passed away on July 13, 1892.

Flash forward to the early 1900s where a vigorous debate raged about the origins of baseball. One camp, led by Albert Spalding, editor of the *Baseball Guide*, argued that the game was purely American in origin. The opposing view was put forth by sportswriter Harry Chadwick. He maintained that the game evolved from British roots and the sport of rounders. Despite his friendship with Spalding, Chadwick scorned the attempts to have Doubleday deemed baseball's inventor. "He means well," Chadwick said of Spalding, "but he don't know."

Henry Chadwick was inducted into the Baseball Hall of Fame by the Veterans Committee in 1938. His plaque reads:

HENRY CHADWICK
BASEBALL'S PREEMINENT PIONEER
WRITER FOR HALF A CENTURY.
INVENTOR OF THE BOX SCORE.
AUTHOR OF THE FIRST RULE-BOOK
IN 1858 CHAIRMAN OF RULES
COMMITTEE IN FIRST NATION-WIDE
BASEBALL ORGANIZATION.

The seven-member Mills Commission was created by Spalding to search out the genesis of the sport. Committee members included Col. A. G. Mills of New York, who played baseball before and during the Civil War and was the fourth president of the National League; Morgan G. Bulkeley, former governor and then U.S. Senator from Connecticut, the National League's first president; Arthur P. Gorman, U.S. Senator from Maryland, a former player; Nicholas E. Young, a longtime player and fifth president of the National League; Alfred J. Reach of Philadelphia and George Wright of Boston, two of the most famous players of their day; and James E. Sullivan, president of the Amateur Athletic Union.

On December 30, 1907, after three years of "study," the group announced that it was young Abner Doubleday who laid out the first baseball diamond in Cooperstown, New York, in 1839. A statement by a "reputable gentleman," octogenarian and former mining engineer from Denver, Abner Graves, was the basis for the findings. Graves claimed that during his youth in Cooperstown in 1839 he saw a Doubleday diagram for a baseball diamond in a pasture that belonged to farmer Elihu Phinney.

"I can well understand," Mills wrote, "how the orderly mind of the embryo West Pointer would devise a scheme for the limiting of the contestants on each side and allotting them to field positions, each with a certain amount of territory."

The committee's final report stated, in part, that "the first scheme for playing baseball, according to the best evidence obtainable to date, was devised by Abner Doubleday at Cooperstown, N.Y. in 1839." The commission also concluded that Doubleday was the first to establish a limit of nine players per team, that he invented the force-out, and that he later traveled about the country singing the praises and explaining the intricacies of the game.

It's such a nice story. It comes complete with Doubleday as Pied Piper, part Johnny Appleseed, and seems to contain the original field of dreams. But it's only one story—and one that is totally untrue.

For one thing, Doubleday, who some say was a relative of Mills, never claimed credit for inventing the game. Truth be told, Doubleday was at West Point that day, not in Cooperstown. When, according to the myth, he was allegedly chalking off foul lines in Cooperstown in 1839, he was actually a student attending classes 100 miles away in West Point. But because he graduated from the Point in 1842 and became a well-known Civil War hero, Abner Doubleday was the perfect model of the man who could have and should have invented baseball.

But he did not. He never spoke of baseball, probably never saw a game. As one writer put it: Doubleday "didn't know a baseball from a kumquat." Truth be told, the myth was spread by an imaginative sporting goods manufacturer seeking to merchandise baseball as a truly American game.

In 1939, Baseball Commissioner Kenesaw Mountain Landis helped orchestrate the celebration of the baseball centennial at Cooperstown. Always adept at such things, he encouraged the accompanying hype and hoopla. The Baseball Hall of Fame had appointed a group to document baseball's origins. They went along with the Mills Commission findings that credited Abner Doubleday with creating the sport in 1839 at Cooperstown, New York.

At this point Bruce Cartwright, who lived in Honolulu and was a grandson of Alexander Cartwright, entered the scene. Armed with his grandfather's diary, clippings, and other documents, he argued passionately that Alexander Cartwright, not Abner Doubleday, was the originator of baseball.

Too much money and effort had been expended preparing to celebrate the "centennial" to call it off. As an accommodation, some would say as balm to soothe Bruce Cartwright, an Alexander Cartwright Day was included in the festivities that inaccurately celebrated Abner Doubleday as the man who invented baseball. Cartwright was also admitted to the Hall of Fame. His plaque reads:

ALEXANDER JOY CARTWRIGHT, JR.
"FATHER OF MODERN BASE BALL."
SET BASES 90 FEET APART.
ESTABLISHED 9 INNINGS AS GAME
AND 9 PLAYERS AS TEAM. ORGANIZED
THE KNICKERBOCKER BASEBALL CLUB
OF N.Y. IN 1845. CARRIED BASEBALL
TO PACIFIC COAST AND HAWAII
IN PIONEER DAYS.

The origins of the game before 1845 are still murky, however. References to early forms of baseball in New York cities such as Rochester and Geneseo in the 1820s have been uncovered. There is some indication that organized clubs played in Philadelphia and the New York City area in the 1830s. There was some early baseball in Massachusetts, New Hampshire, Vermont, and other northeastern states. Most of these games, however, bore little resemblance to today's game.

BASEBALL'S EARLY EVOLUTION

Alexander Cartwright's game—with its first written rules—was a "refined" version of "town ball," "goal ball," "baste ball," the "Massachusetts game," and other bat-and-ball sports, all of which derived from the English games of rounders and cricket.

A strict code of personal behavior characterized the atmosphere of those early baseball teams. Unlike the folk games—the pickup games that had preceded Cartwright's game—the new game was a stylized affair, a gentlemen's game. Only those spectators invited by the competing clubs bore witness to the early baseball games. Ladies were comfortably seated in the shade of tents; and tea, crackers, and other polite refreshments were made available for all spectators.

The purpose of the game was to allow the batter to hit; pitchers obliged by throwing the ball where the batter requested it. Bunting was frowned upon. Players trapped off base allowed themselves to be politely tagged out. Unruliness on the part of players was discouraged; fines were levied against players who disobeyed their captain, argued with the umpire, or resorted to profanity.

Home teams treated visiting teams to a gala dinner after games, and social gatherings between clubs that included wives and girl friends highlighted the off-season. Baseball was indeed a game for gentlemen. It was also a restricted game for a time limited to amateurs and the upper social class.

By 1856, there were nearly 50 baseball clubs in and around Manhattan. On March 10, 1857, the Knickerbockers and 15 other teams banded together, forming the National Association of Base Ball Players. The league changed and codified some of the rules. There would now be only nine men on a side, bases would be 90 feet apart, the umpire was given the power to call strikes, and no one was allowed to catch the ball in his cap. More important, baseball was to remain an amateur game: no player was ever to be paid.

The NABBP attempted to keep the genteel climate of the game in force. Gambling at games was banned. Admission fees to games became more common as a way of "attracting" a better class and less violence. Professionals and those players who were deemed not to be of the right social standing were barred. Some but not all of the NABBP teams even refused to compete against clubs they regarded as their social inferiors. However, the most telling change in the state of organized baseball was revealed in the fact that not one of the NABBP's six original officers was a representative of Cartwright's old Knickerbocker club.

Baseball in New York spread quickly. Teams formed in all areas of the city. More and more teams were organized—the Gothams, Eagles, Eckfords Excelsiors, etc. Brooklyn especially became known as the "City of Baseball Clubs." In December 1856, the *New York Mercury* declared the game the "National Pastime." That declaration was hyperbole, standard newspaperspeak for the time.

By 1858, trains made their way to Long Island to witness games at the Fashion Race Course. It was there that 4,000 spectators were on hand for the All–New York vs. All-Brooklyn series. This three-game series marked the first time that baseball charged an admission fee at the gate—50 cents—with proceeds benefiting New York–area fire department charities.

By the late 1850s, baseball had become more democratized and was daily increasing in popularity against its main rival, cricket, whose slowness and lengthy playing time doomed it as a major American sport. Unlike cricket, baseball, in Mark Twain's words, was "the very symbol, the outward and visible expression of the drive and push and rush and struggle of the raging, tearing, booming nineteenth century."

By 1860, the New York game—or as some called it, "the manly" version of baseball—spread to Maine and had become established in such places as New Orleans, Oregon, and California. Baseball was no longer a reserved genteel competition, a sport only for men of manners. Bigger and bigger crowds came to see the matches. Foul lines were a terrific innovation, making it safe for spectators but also enabling them to be close to the action.

Sixty clubs had joined the association, including teams from as far away as St. Louis and Chicago. That 1860 season, the Excelsiors of Brooklyn were the first club to go on the road. They triumphed over teams in Albany, Troy, Buffalo, Rochester, and Newburgh. News of these victories was carried over telegraph lines across the nation, stoking the baseball fever. In Baltimore, Wilmington, and Philadelphia, thousands came out to see them play.

A storied figure of that era was Jim Creighton, star of the Brooklyn Excelsiors and Brooklyn Stars. Allegedly the first professional player, the first real master of the game, he reportedly was the first pitcher who harnessed speed and control. Creighton also threw a pitch described as a "speedball." That nifty pitch was delivered to the plate with Creighton skillfully disguising the fact he snapped his wrist—a rules violation back then. The shifty Creighton also featured a "slowball" that he paired with his "speedball." The combination baffled batters and brought him much fame; several little town teams were so smitten with his accomplishments that they named themselves "Creighton."

Unfortunately, the Jim Creighton story had a very tragic ending. In 1862, he swung his bat with all his might and homered. But the ferociousness of that swing ruptured his bladder. Creighton died a few days later at age 21. He was acclaimed in his obituary as "one of the best players in the Union."

By 1862, about 200 junior and senior teams played baseball in the New York City metropolitan area and northern New Jersey. Other urban regions formed leagues of their own—town ball was their game. But it was the "New York Game" that laid down the style of baseball to come.

Legend reports on baseball's rural roots. Reality underscores the fact that early baseball was an urban phenomenon.

Fans—they were called "cranks"—engaged in all types of outrageous behavior: heckling umpires, razzing players, even rioting. For the fans, it was suggested, baseball was not simply a matter of life and death—it was more important than that. The final stanza of "Casey at the Bat" epitomized the emotional pull of the sport:

> Oh! somewhere in this favored land the sun is shining bright;
> The band is playing somewhere, and somewhere hearts are light.
> And somewhere men are laughing, and somewhere children shout
> But there is no joy in Mudville—mighty Casey has Struck Out.

Casey notwithstanding, baseball rolled on. Even the great catastrophe of the Civil War did not impede the growth of the game. In fact, the sport was spurred on by it. Soldiers of the Blue and the Gray used it as a break and diversion from battlefield tensions.

"Modern baseball had been born in the brain of an American soldier. It received its baptism in the bloody days of our Nation's direst danger. It had its early evolution when soldiers, North and South, were striving to forget their foes by cultivating, through this grand game, fraternal friendship with comrades in arms."

—Albert Spalding

George Putnam, a Union soldier stationed in Texas, had a vivid memory of a game played between the lines: "Suddenly," he said, "there came a scattering fire of which the three outfielders caught the brunt; the center field was hit and was captured, the left and right field managed to get back into our lines. The attack . . . was repelled without serious difficulty, but we had lost not only our center field, but . . . the only baseball in Alexandria, Texas."

On Christmas Day in 1862, approximately 40,000 troops watched games of baseball. In prison camps, Union prisoners passed the time playing the game, even challenging their Confederate captors in contests of baseball skill. It was reported that President Abraham Lincoln and his son watched games played behind the White House.

FACTOID

Baseball cards, first packaged with tobacco products in 1886 by Virginia's Allen & Ginter Company, gave many a look at the new baseball heroes, a look that they might never have had in person.

A few of the games that had been recorded for historical significance either by participants or observers are listed in table 1. (For

Table 1. Civil War Baseball Games

Date	Cause	Participants	Notables
1862	Union	Trainees from 13th Massachusetts and 51st Pennsylvania vs. themselves	Games were played evenings on the drilling field in many training camps prior to deployment.
1862	Union	165th New York Infantry (Second Duryea's Zouaves) vs. New York Regiment All-Star nine	Perhaps one of the most famous of all Civil War games, this one was witnessed by 40,000 troops.
1862	Union	The "Irish Brigade" vs. themselves	Confederate sentries stationed across the Chickahominy River watched Union games played during General McClellan's march to Richmond.
1862	Union	57th New York vs. 69th New York	Incoming Confederate cannon fire ended this game abruptly.
1862	Union	2nd Brigade, 2nd Division, Army of the Potomac vs. selected members of the "Honey Run Club" team	Members of both the brigade and the 1859 champions practiced regularly throughout the war.
1863	Confederate	24th Alabama vs. themselves	Rebels played daily while stationed in wait for the advancing Federal Army led by General William Tecumseh Sherman.
1863	Union	26th Pennsylvania vs. 22nd Massachusetts vs. 13th New York vs. 62nd New York Volunteers	All four regiments met for games, but disputed the differences between the Massachusetts and New York rules.

Year	Side	Teams	Notes
1863	Union	13th Massachusetts and 1st Rhode Island Light Artillery vs. misc. Army	Both teams had recorded so many victories, many felt that they were capable of beating any professional team of the late 1800s.
1863	Union	1st New Jersey Artillery, Battery B vs. themselves	First printed drawing published of a baseball game, played before the Battle of Chancellorsville.
1863	Union	Union soldiers encamped in Alexandria, Texas	During this game, the camp was attacked, resulting in the loss of the center fielder and the ball.
1864	Union	2nd New Jersey Volunteers vs. 77th New York Volunteers All-Star nine	Billed as another big game, newspapers openly criticized the 77th after a no-show.
1864	Union	1st New Jersey Artillery vs. 10th Massachusetts Infantry	*New York Clipper* newspaper covered the game at Brandy Station. New Jersey lost 13–15.
1864	Confederate	11th Mississippi POWs at Union Prison Camp in Sandusky, Ohio (Confederate Club vs. Southerners)	One game recorded, ended with the Confederates winning 19–11.
1865	Both	Union and Confederate soldiers from both the Army of the Potomac and the Army of Northern Virginia	Following General Robert E. Lee's surrender at Appomattox Courthouse, soldiers from both sides played to pass the time.
1866	Union	POWs detained at the Confederate Prison Camp in Salisbury, North Carolina	Despite pleasant accounts of baseball early on, many players later died due to overcrowded conditions.

simplicity, all forms of the game including "town ball" and "round-ball" will be referred to as baseball.)

Postwar baseball boomed. Baseball clubs were formed on college campuses throughout the United States. But despite the sport's popularity, there were major problems and scandals. In 1866, the Philadelphia Athletics openly paid three players $20 a week. Lipman E. ("Lip") Pike, the first great Jewish baseball player, became baseball's first professional that season when Philly signed him first and put him at third base. Many other players were on payrolls in a more disguised manner.

One egregious example of this practice was engaged in by New York's Tammany Hall boss William Marcy Tweed, who was also president of the New York Mutuals from 1860 to 1871. All his baseball players were classified as sweepers or clerks on the New York City payroll—a classification that cost the taxpayers of New York City $30,000 annually.

"Hippodroming" of games became the vogue in some quarters. That was the practice of players consorting with gamblers to fix scores or games. At some ballparks, gamblers were highly visible out in the open, quoting odds, taking bets, collecting money. The Troy (New York) Haymakers were reportedly under the total control of gamblers. Six-shooters were fired in games in California just as a fielder was about to camp under a fly ball. The guns, it was understood, were on the side of the team that was batting. In some games where much money had been wagered, fans flocked out onto the field to prevent a loss to the team they had backed with their pocketbooks.

"So common has betting become," noted *Harper's Weekly*, "that the most respectable clubs in the country indulge in it to a highly culpable degree, and so common . . . the tricks by which games have been 'sold' for the benefit of gamblers that the most respectable participants have been suspected of baseness."

"Revolving" was another problem that drew daily criticism from the newspapers of the time. It was a practice that witnessed players moving from team to team—in effect, selling their services to the highest bidder. One notorious example was the case of William Fischer. Agreeing to perform for the Philadelphia Athletics after being rewarded by the team with a brand-new suit of clothes, a job, room and board, and a $15 bonus, Fischer left the team in the lurch after a few days. He then "revolved" with his new suit and his bonus money to the Cubs of Chicago, who had offered a better deal for his services.

By the final years of the 1860s, "professionals" were on the rosters of most of the leading teams of the day: the Haymakers, the Brooklyn Atlantics, the Mutuals, the Athletics, the Chicago White Stockings, the Lansingburgh (New York) Unions, the Buckeyes of Cincinnati, and the Marylands of Baltimore.

Baseball became more and more the American game, a sport played throughout the length and breadth of the country, a game that famed orator Clarence Darrow mused about when recalling his growing-up years in a small town in Ohio as "the one unalloyed joy in life."

Heated rivalries between eastern and western teams accentuated the excitement of baseball during the 1860s. Frenetic sectional competition was personified by the Washington Nationals of 1867, who in their tour of the West humbled all the teams they encountered. Then Washington arrived in Chicago to oppose the Forest City Club of Rockford, Illinois. Upholding western pride, Forest City, behind the pitching of young Albert Spalding, outlasted Washington 29–23 in the game played at Dexter Park. Watches, jewelry, and other gifts were bestowed on the Rockford nine by the town's grateful citizens. The celebration and merriment went on for more than a week. Finally, some would say, embarrassingly, all the merrymaking came to an end when the Washington Nationals issued an open letter offering the disclaimer that they were not the national champions.

BLACK BASEBALL

On a shimmering October day in 1867, nine Harrisburg men squared off against nine visiting Philadelphians in "a match game of ball" that grew out of a friendly invitation by the secretary of the Monrovia Base Ball Club of Harrisburg to the newly formed Philadelphia Pythians. The visiting Pythians outscored the hometown Monrovians, 59–27, in this historic game and would shortly be involved in events that would shape the game of baseball for the next century. This game, however, was historic for Harrisburg because it is the first recorded match between an all-black Harrisburg baseball team and an all-black visiting team.

Two years later, on September 18, 1869, the Pythians became the first all-black team to play an exhibition game against an all-white team. The Pythians defeated the City Items, 27–17.

A few months after the Monrovians–Pythians game, the Philadelphia club attempted to gain admission into the National Association of Base Ball Players. The application was rejected by the league, which said: "If colored clubs were admitted there would be in all probability some division of feeling, whereas, by excluding them no injury could result to anyone." The *Philadelphia Inquirer* reported that the association "declared itself against the admission of any clubs composed of colored men, and any white club having colored members."

The Mutuals, an African-American team that had been formed consisting primarily of government clerks, went on tour in September 1870. The team traveled to Baltimore and Lockport, Maryland, and Niagara Falls, Buffalo, Rochester, Utica, Canajoharie, and Troy, New York. They won all eight games, outscoring their opponents by an average score of 47–13. The following August, the Mutuals played the Pythians of Philadelphia on the grounds of the Athletics Club, losing twice, 20–15 and 17–16. At the time, the Pythians and Mutuals were regarded as the two best black teams in the nation.

"THE FIRST PROFESSIONAL BASEBALL TEAM"

The first truly professional team was the Cincinnati Red Stockings, established in 1869. It was not that they were the first team of paid players; it was just that they were the first team that publicly announced that its players were paid. Before the Red Stockings, the rival club in Cincinnati, the Buckeyes, had been giving players steady wages. Financing for the Red Stockings came from a group of Ohio investors.

Organized in 1867 by the aptly named Aaron B. Champion, 26, the Cincinnati team was entrusted to the hands of English-born Harry Wright, a former jeweler and cricket player, a veteran of a decade of top-drawer baseball competition. Wright had come to the United States when his father, a famous cricket player, was hired by the fashionable St. George Cricket Club in New York. The Wright brothers, Harry, George, and Sam, took up the game of baseball to the chagrin of their cricket-loving dad.

1867 CINCINNATI BASE BALL CLUB ROSTER
John McLean, Catcher
J. Wayne Neff, First Base
Bellemy Storer, Second Base
Dave Schwartz, Third Base
John C. How, Shortstop
Moses Grant, Left Field
J. Williams Johnson, Center Field
Gerald Ellard, Right Field
Harry Wright, Pitcher
William Worthington, Scorer

Champion looked upon the Red Stockings as a way to promote the city of Cincinnati, its products and services. And Champion looked upon Harry Wright as scout, recruiter, player, and manager—as a man to get a job done.

Harry Wright was not bashful to announce that he knew a few things about sports. Baseball's popularity throughout the United

States convinced Wright that people who happily dole out "seventy-five cents to one dollar to go to the theatre, prefer base ball to theatricals."

The total payroll for the 1869 season for the Red Stockings was $9,300. Salaries covered the period from March to November and ranged from $800 to a high of $1,400 for brother George Wright. The lone sub picked up $600. The Red Stockings became the first team to travel across the United States with its players signed and bound to the club for the entire season.

Only one member of the team actually came from Cincinnati, despite the hometown hype. Most players were young New Yorkers from varying professions, including hat making, insurance sales, bookkeeping, and piano making, who had made their reputations playing on successful amateur teams.

The Red Stockings were referred to as a "picked nine," which might have been an exaggeration—but it was a nine picked by Harry Wright. The only native of Cincinnati on the team was first baseman Charlie Gould, nicknamed the "bushel basket" because of his ability to snare baseballs. Others included Wright; his brother George, star shortstop, obtained from the Morrisania Unions of New York; third baseman Fred Waterman; outfielders Asa Brainard, Dave Birdsall, and Andy Leonard; pitcher Cal McVey; second baseman Cal Sweasy; and catcher Doug Allison. Harry Wright doubled as a relief pitcher, and Dick Hurley, appropriated from the Buckeyes of Cincinnati, functioned as a utility player.

A shrewd promoter, Harry Wright insisted on his team wearing bright red stockings to set off their white flannel shirts and pants and dark Oxford shoes. The garb was a bit outlandish for the time, but the outfit attracted attention. That, of course, was what Wright and Chapman were after.

Harry Wright, a stern taskmaster, went about drilling the team, mandating work habits, insisting players be businesslike on the field, admonishing them on diet, drink, tobacco, and clean living. Wright's team was prepared to take on all comers—if the price was right—and take on all comers they did, while the Queen City team pocketed a hefty share of the gate receipts.

Winners of their first 17 games, the team from the West confronted the Mutuals on June 14, 1869, before 8,000 fans at the Union Grounds in Brooklyn. The Red Stockings prevailed 4–2 over the tough eastern team. That victory was a pivotal moment in the fortunes of the Red Stockings, for from that triumph on, opponents realized the Cincinnati team was not a sideshow but a main event.

More high moments existed for the Red Stockings like the big paydays in New York City and Philadelphia where over 23,000 spectators witnessed their six-game series in the Big Apple and almost 15,000 assembled for a game in Philadelphia. But there were washouts figuratively and literally in other places. Sawdust and brooms applied to the wet places on the field in Rochester sopped up rainy-day problems there. In Syracuse, Wright's baseballers had to contend with a ballpark ready for the wrecker's ball, 12-inch-high grass, and a live-pigeon shoot being staged on the field. Syracuse was a non-payday.

That season the Cincinnati Red Stockings played baseball throughout the Northeast and West, traveling 11,000 miles. The team won 57 games and recorded one disputed tie against the Troy Haymakers. On June 26, the team had a private audience in Washington with President Ulysses S. Grant, who complimented the western "Cinderella" club for its skills and winning ways.

In September, they journeyed across the country on the newly completed transcontinental railroad, playing a series of games in California. During the trip, nearly 200,000 fans attended the games.

Photographs of the "picked nine," serious-looking young men with beards and sideburns, were everywhere. The stock photographs captured the facade but not the tone of the team. Despite Wright's best efforts, excessive alcohol consumption, a penchant for skipping practices and missing trains, and an eccentric and individualistic attitude characterized the merry band of players, who swept the country, along with their catchy theme song:

> We are a band of baseball players
> From Cincinnati city.
> We come to toss the ball around

And sing to you our ditty
And if you listen to the song
We are about to sing,
We'll tell you all about baseball
And make the welkin ring.
The ladies want to know
Who are those gallant men in
Stockings red, they'd like to know.

FACTOID

Trouncing the Mutual Green Stockings of New York 17–8, the Red Stockings won their 60th game without a loss before 7,000 Cincinnati fans who shuddered against the cold weather on November 5th.

At season's end, feted and praised in a lavish homecoming, the Red Stockings were presented with a 27-foot bat by the Cincinnati Lumber Company—a symbol of their on-the-field accomplishments. "I'd rather be president of the Cincinnati Baseball Club," bragged Champion, "than president of the United States."

"Glory," one proud Cincinnati booster said, "I don't know anything about baseball or town ball, nowadays, but it does me good to see those fellows. They've done something to add to the glory of our city. They advertised the city, advertised us, sir, and helped our business."

The Red Stockings had a winning first season—65 wins and no losses—but made a profit of only $1.39. Nevertheless, in the final balance sheet of baseball doings for 1869, the Red Stockings of Cincinnati managed to have a tremendous impact on the state of baseball in America. "They met with such remarkable success in that year," noted famed baseball journalist Harry Chadwick, "that their exploits are noteworthy in the history of the game."

Harry Wright was now an icon. The *Cincinnati Enquirer* reported: "He eats base-ball, breathes base-ball, thinks base-ball, dreams base-ball, and incorporates base-ball in his prayers."

Part of the impact of the Red Stockings was on other cities that wanted a baseball champion to represent them. Cincinnati's success made it sunset time for the amateur in baseball and dawn for professionalism. An editorial in the *Chicago Tribune*, miffed because it was constantly reporting on the one-sided losses of the local team, reflected the mood of the time. It called for "a representative club; an organization as great as her [Chicago's] enterprise and wealth, one that will not allow the second-rate clubs of every village in the Northwest to carry away the honors in baseball."

The Red Stockings had triggered a trend. In Chicago, civic pride enabled $20,000 to be raised to organize a strong professional team, and advertisements were placed soliciting the efforts of topflight players. In other cities the same type of enterprising effort was launched. Teams that had previously competed wearing the mask of amateurism now would become full-fledged professional organizations.

On March 7, 1870, the Cincinnati Red Stockings began an eight-month tour of the Midwest and East. The Red Stockings, the best team in all of baseball, kept on rolling over the opposition in 1870. By early June their winning streak had reached 84 straight triumphs—27 in a row that season.

Then on June 14th, they came up against the Brooklyn Atlantics at the Capitoline Grounds in Brooklyn. It was hailed as the greatest game of the year. It was to be the most historic game of 19th-century baseball.

The heavily favored Cincy aggregation on that steamy day sported knickers, vivid red wool stockings, and shirts emblazoned with an old English "C." The Atlantics wore caps of light buff linen, long blue trousers, and shirts with "A" stitched on the chest. An excited and noisy Brooklyn crowd that numbered in estimates that ranged all the way to 20,000 showed up to watch the action.

George "the Charmer" Zettlein, the top fastball pitcher of the time, and Bob "Death to Flying Things" Ferguson formed the battery for the Atlantics. Stationed at second base was Lipman Pike, the first top-notch Jewish ballplayer. In 1858, a week after his bar mitzvah, he appeared in a box score. That was the least of his accomplishments.

The very speedy Pike also raced 100 yards against a Standardbred horse for $200—and won.

The Reds were ahead 3–0 after three innings. At the end of nine innings, the score was tied 5–5. Back then, draws were declared if the score was tied at the end of the regulation nine innings. The Brooklyn Atlantics would have settled for that. But as the story goes, Harry Wright checked with Henry Chadwick who was at the game. The well-known amateur statistician and professional baseball historian maintained that the game should go to extra innings.

With the Atlantics already changing clothes in their locker room, with fans milling about on the playing field, Aaron Champion told Harry Wright to have the Red Stockings play on. Order was restored and the teams did indeed play on.

Cincy scored twice in the top of the 11th inning. It seemed over, but the Atlantics were not done. In the bottom of the 11th, with ace Asa Brainard on the mound for Cincinnati, the Atlantics tied the game with a single, a wild pitch, then two more hits. There was only one out for the Atlantics. They had a runner, Bob Ferguson, on first base. The next batter George Zettlein tapped a grounder to first base. Charlie Gould, the Red Stockings' first baseman, allowed the ball to play him—it bounced between his legs. Ferguson sped home.

"From 12,000 to 15,200 people passed into the inclosure [*sic*] to witness the sport and we are sorry to say that the crowd was boisterous and noisy and greatly marred the pleasure of the game for those who wanted to look on quietly. The Red Stockings were not treated with the courtesy they had hitherto received, and for the first time, and we trust, the last, partisan feeling was allowed to display itself."

—*Harper's Weekly*

The 8–7 come-from-behind victory for the Atlantics triggered celebration turning the partisan crowd wild, some said berserk. Running a gauntlet of catcalls, jeers, and projectiles, the defeated and dejected Red Stockings were fortunate to escape the playing field and the borough of Brooklyn with their lives.

"Within an hour," one newspaper reported, "the result had been telegraphed to every city, town in the United States. Maybe even to Los Angeles."

When Champion finally made it to the safety of his hotel room, he collapsed in tears. Recovered, he sent off a telegram to the *Commercial:* "Atlantics 8 Cincinnati 7. The finest game ever played. Our boys did nobly but fortune was against us. Though beaten, not disgraced."

Incredibly, the defeat did disgrace the greatest team in the land and destroyed some of the mystique of the Red Stockings. Jaded fans did not flock to games as they previously had. Investors began to withdraw from the scene. The *Cincinnati Gazette* joined in the bashing spree: "The baseball mania has run its course. It has no future as a professional endeavor."

Then the Red Stockings experienced another defeat—this time to Chicago. Champion was forced out of the presidency by a revolt of Cincinnati stockholders. Penny-pinching became the order of the day as a buffer against declining attendance.

With money tight, and Champion still on the scene but lacking the old power, that 1870 season was the last grand hurrah for the Cincinnati Red Stockings. Before the year was over, the club broke up. The Wright brothers, Harry and George, moved on with some of the best Cincinnati players and set up shop in Boston in the National Association of Professional Baseball Players. It was there they would inaugurate another baseball dynasty—the Boston Red Stockings.

FACTOID

In 1870, Harvard University's baseball club embarked on a 43-day, 25-game tour that went as far as St. Louis. Concurrent with that, the nation's top seven to eight clubs were totaling approximately $100,000 in admission receipts.

THE NATIONAL ASSOCIATION

The National Association was founded on March 17, 1871—St. Patrick's Day—at Collier's Cafe on Broadway and 13th Street in New York City. The organization's charter members included the Boston Red Stockings, Chicago White Stockings, Cleveland Forest Citys, Fort Wayne Kekiongas, New York Mutuals, Philadelphia Athletics, Rockford Forest Citys, Troy Haymakers, and Washington Olympics. The Eckfords of Brooklyn attended the meeting but declined to participate that first National Association season, not wishing to chance losing the $10 admission fee. When the Kekiongas dropped out of the league in midsummer, the Eckfords took their place. A 22–7 record enabled the Philadelphia Athletics to win the first National Association championship. Chicago took second place. The Red Stockings, hampered by injuries, wound up third in 1871.

However, from 1872 to 1875 Harry Wright's Red Stockings hit their stride, winning three championships and utterly dominating the National Association. One of the great stars Harry Wright could always rely on was his younger brother George. A bushy-mustached 150-pounder filled with verve and baseball skills, George batted .409, .336, .378, .345, and .337 with Boston. He was one of the major reasons for the Red Stockings' success.

"First each man runs a quarter of a mile, then gentle exercise upon the horizontal bar is taken, after which a trial at vaulting on the vaulting bar is indulged; then a series of Indian Club swinging, followed by the whole team pulling about one mile on the rowing apparatus. After all this, the club retires to a bowling alley where they pass and strike balls.

—Description in the *New York Sunday Mercury* of the New Haven club's preparation for an upcoming season

Another even more significant reason for Boston's winning ways was pitcher Albert Goodwill Spalding, possessor of a herky-jerk underhand delivery out of which came fastball after fastball. In five seasons with Boston, Spalding won 207 games, lost just 56. In 1875 his record was an eye-popping 57–5.

Wright's team was a colossus astride the National Association. In 1875, the Red Stockings posted an incredible 71–8 record and lost just one game on their home field. That 1875 season the top four hitters in the National Association were from Boston; 8 of the top 20 batters were Red Stockings. Only Harry Wright averaged less than a hit a game that year, and he was almost washed up. With Albert Spalding holding the other teams down and with Boston batters racking up opposing pitchers, it was no contest. The Red Stockings finished 15 games ahead of the pack.

Other teams in the league were hapless. Just five of them played at a .500 clip that 1875 season. The Brooklyn team was a joke with a 2–42 record; Keokuk, Iowa, managed just one triumph in 13 games and left the league. Four other teams combined for a record of 17–88 and also dropped out of the National Association.

Afflicted with domination by the Red Stockings, a team that demoralized and unbalanced the competition (the National Association was called Harry Wright's league); with heavy drinking by many players (it was called "lushing" even back then); with the throwing of games (hippodroming); with players moving at will from team to team (revolving); with few clubs actually making money and others simply refusing to complete their schedules—the five-year-old league saw 25 different clubs come and go. With a total lack of leadership, the National Association was a mess.

The game of baseball in the 1860s and 1870s was also a mess. Uniformity was not its hallmark. It was played with an oversized ball, pitched underhanded to the batter. There were times that the ball was so "rubberized" that it high-bounced its way in the outfield over the head of a fielder. Mushiness other times characterized the ball and made it difficult for a batter to even hit it out of the infield. Bats came in various lengths and weights.

Gloves for fielders did not exist, except that catchers sometimes had a regular leather glove with the fingers cut off. Scores could be ridiculous. A case in point: Red Stockings 103, Buckeyes 8. The Buckeyes folded after that game.

The existence of but one umpire was an inducement and encouragement for tricks of all kinds, like a player distracting him so that a teammate was able to make a catch with his cap—an illegal move. Rules violations ruled the game. Example: rules mandated the ball be pitched from "below the belt." Pitchers wore belts just below their armpits. "Clubhouse lawyers" were on most rosters, specialists knowledgeable about written rules and all kinds of ways around them.

The general messy state of affairs—on the field, off the field, organizationally, and personality-wise in baseball—set the stage for the entrance of colorful William A. Hulbert, born in Burlington Flats, New York, just 13 miles west of Cooperstown. In 1870, the coal magnate had become a charter stockholder of the Chicago White Stockings of the National Association. "I'd rather be a lamppost in Chicago," he had bragged, "than a millionaire elsewhere. I'll take control of this game of baseball away from the easterners."

FACTOID

A 19th-century pitcher would be assigned the duty of handling the gate for road games he wasn't starting. The pitcher would watch the gates, count the tickets, and ensure that his team obtained appropriate share of receipts.

When Boston made its first trip to Chicago in 1875, Hulbert, poised to become club president, arranged a private meeting with the highly successful but also highly ambitious Albert Spalding. "You've no business playing in Boston," Hulbert informed Spalding. "You're a western boy and should be playing here. If you come to Chicago, you can be captain and manager of the team at $4,000 a year and I'll take over the presidency and we'll give those easterners the fight of their lives."

The idea appealed to Spalding. Although he was a big star in Boston, he was a man always anxious to better his station in life. "You bet, I'll come to Chicago," Spalding told Hulbert. "And I'll bring a team of pennant winners along with me—Ross Barnes, Cal McVey, and Deacon White. The people call us the Big Four, but the owners don't pay us very well. A championship team should be paid like champions. "

The Big Four announced their plans, to the fury of the cranks of Boston. "You seceders," some of the unhappy fans screamed. "Your White Stockings will get soiled in Chicago."

Hulbert, never afraid of being called an overreacher, also signed the young Philadelphia phenom Cap Anson to a contract for 1876. And with the "Big Four" and Anson in the fold, William Ambrose Hulbert was primed for battle.

THE NATIONAL LEAGUE

By 1876, the National Association was in trouble. Hulbert seized the opportunity to step in. In secrecy, he quickly had lured five of the best players on Association teams to Chicago. National Association moguls, miffed by all of Hulbert's maneuverings, began to set plans in motion to eject the Chicagoan and his White Stockings from the league. The resourceful Hulbert arranged a meeting with Spalding to plan a counterattack strategy.

"Mr. Hulbert and I were in a serious discussion about what we should do," Spalding recalled. "For a few moments I noticed that he was engrossed in deep thought. 'Spalding, I have a new scheme. Let us anticipate the eastern cusses and organize a new association before the March meeting, and then we shall see who shall do the expelling.'"

On February 2, 1876, a great storm lashed the Atlantic seaboard. A 70-mile-an-hour gale ravaged the New York City area and business was brought to a standstill. Most people stayed at home.

William A. Hulbert of Chicago was a long way from home. He peered out the window of his room at the fashionable Grand Central Hotel in Manhattan and contemplated the fury of nature. The president of the Chicago baseball team of the National Association had traveled to New York City to meet with four easterners determined to convince them of the great sporting and financial future of baseball, a future he believed was there for the taking if they would only go along with his vision.

A month before in Louisville, the ambitious and flamboyant 44-year-old Hulbert had met secretly with representatives of St. Louis, Cincinnati, and Louisville. He had convinced them of the wisdom of forming a new baseball league that would stem what he called the decline of the game.

While the wind howled and steeples fell in New York City, Hulbert first shrewdly conferred privately for a half hour with representatives of each of the eastern clubs. Then he gathered together the entire aggregation in a second-floor meeting room in the Grand Central Hotel.

With great theatrical flourish, Hulbert went to the door once all the representatives were settled. He turned the key in the lock and then made a great show of depositing it in his pocket. "Do not be alarmed, gentlemen." He smiled. "I merely took the precaution of seeing that there will not be any intrusion from the outside. There is some business that has to be finished and no one will leave this room until I have explained everything."

The easterners representing Boston, Hartford, New York City, and Philadelphia listened as Hulbert patiently explained that he had been granted the power of attorney from the four western clubs to create a new baseball organization. Then he launched into a bitter tirade about the low state of baseball. A businessman who had never played baseball, Hulbert was appalled at the player-controlled state of the National Association of Professional Baseball Players, a league that was run largely by the players.

"Inflated salaries," Hulbert continued, telling the eastern representatives what they knew well, "players jumping from team to team during the season, gambling scandals, team imbalance, incomplete schedules—all of these can and will be wiped away."

Hulbert was not just holding forth but was accurately outlining many of the vexing problems of National Association baseball: teams located in cities of different sizes, creating disjointed demographics from which to draw. No specific schedule of games. Heavy gambling action and bookmakers flourishing with their booths out in the open. Players allegedly fixing games for the right price. Fracases, fights, and near-riots sometimes accompanying the baseball action.

"I propose," Hulbert spoke in a loud and impassioned voice, "a closed corporation" of baseball. "Why should we be losing money when we represent a game that people love?" The men whom Hulbert had once disparagingly referred to as "eastern cusses" agreed with his complaints and reasoning. They told him to go on with his presentation. Hulbert explained that the new league he envisioned would be called the National League of Professional Base Ball Clubs. In an age of Carnegie, Rockefeller, Vanderbilt, and Gould, that name was appropriate. It would be a league of clubs—not players. For the first time, baseball would become a management–labor situation, with club owners and administrators running the show and players now cast in the role of employees.

Hulbert had caught the easterners off guard when he locked the door on them. Now he astonished them when he unveiled a 13-point constitution and a player's contract for the new league. Both had been created by Hulbert and Albert Spalding, a businessman as well as an athlete, who looked upon the formation of the new league as a way to give management the upper hand—in his phrase "in the irrepressible conflicts between Labor and Capital."

Constitutional objectives of the new league were "first, to encourage, foster and elevate the game of baseball; second, to enact and enforce proper rules for the exhibition and conduct of the game; third, to make base ball playing respectable and honorable." At the heart of the constitution was the principle that baseball be a profit-making venture; the day of the sport operating as a hobby for status-seeking gentlemen belonged in the past, in Hulbert's view.

Agreement was reached on "territorial rights"—the establishment of but one franchise representing a city of at least 75,000 in population. League members were banned from competing against nonleague teams. New applicants for a franchise would have to be voted in by current club owners and two "blackballs would bar an applicant."

All teams would be required to complete their entire league schedule. Annual dues would be $100—10 times the amount assessed by the National Association. To promote and enhance a lofty and moral image, the constitution specified that Sunday baseball was prohibited, sale of alcohol would not be allowed on clubs' grounds, and gambling of any sort would be illegal. Provisions were also made for police protection. Players would not be permitted to fraternize with fans, and unruly spectators would be subject to ejection from the ballpark by the umpire.

The transfer of power from the players to the owners was the most revolutionary aspect of the constitution. Players would now be tightly bound to their clubs. The lessons of the past—of athletes moving about by whim or responding to the price of the highest bidder—had been painfully absorbed. The Boston Red Stockings, for example, had became a highly successful National Association club by stocking its roster with the best available talent because it paid the highest salaries—about $2,000 per player, a hefty sum for those days.

Additional National League constitutional provisions gave a club the power to expel a player from the league and to create a new type of contract, requiring players to be accountable to all rules laid down by the club. In effect, the constitution was a blank check for the owners providing them with total control of the management, regulation, and resolution of every possible dispute.

Other modern features of the new National League, aimed at making the game of professional baseball less rowdy and more organized, included provisions for paying umpires $5 a game, for permitting only the captain of a team to dispute an umpire's decisions, for scheduling games, and for setting uniform admission prices.

In an age of big business growth the new league was in step with the times. Although its structure was primitive, the National League would nevertheless persevere and set a precedent for all sports teams of the 20th century. In theory and in practice the National League would be a loosely organized cartel—a closed corporation designed to restrict competition among other franchises for players. In essence, the aim of the National League of Professional Base Ball Clubs was to become the only game in town.

William Ambrose Hulbert had a good head for figures and explained to the eastern representatives that the new league would play a highly organized 70-game schedule. The eight charter National League clubs would be Chicago, Boston, New York, Philadelphia, Hartford, Cincinnati, St. Louis, and Louisville. Each of these teams would play 10 games against every other team. The one that won the most games would win the championship and an emblem of victory—a flag. That pennant would cost no more than $100, but it would symbolize the National League champ.

After the eastern representatives approved the 13 points of the new National League constitution, a five-man committee was elected to run the league. A well-known politician, Morgan G. Bulkeley of Hartford, was chosen as president after Hulbert declined the post and supported the Connecticut man.

Then Hulbert prevailed on each delegate to sign a statement that denigrated the National Association for insidious abuses "growing out of an imperfect and unsystematized code." The last order of business was a notice sent out to newspapers after the day-long meeting at the Grand Central Hotel. The notice declared that eight teams had withdrawn from the National Association and had formed the National League of Professional Base Ball Clubs.

Although a significant event in the history of sports had taken place, three days passed before one of the New York City morning newspapers reported what had taken place. Under the heading "Sporting," the news of the new league was preceded by a paragraph about the cancellation of the Savannah Jockey Club's races of the previous day and a report on pigeon shooting lengthier than the news about the new league.

History marks the year 1876 as an American centennial, a time when Ulysses S. Grant was president, when P. T. Barnum was all the rage, when Alexander Graham Bell invented the telephone. It was also the time when the National League came full flower into the world.

The new league was not an altruistic endeavor created by a few honorable men to salvage the sport of baseball, to transform it into the true national pastime and make it "respectable." It was a power play on the part of Hulbert—a self-serving economic power play that worked magnificently.

Professional baseball players were totally taken by surprise and so was the National Association. At a March meeting, the old league attempted to fight back, to reorganize. The efforts were not successful, and the National Association faded into history.

Newspapers debated the fate of the failed National Association and the merits of the new league. Eastern publications, especially those from towns the National League had chosen to pass over, attacked Hulbert.

The *Chicago Tribune*, not totally unbiased where Hulbert was concerned, had dispatched a writer to cover the meeting of moguls in the Grand Central Hotel. The writer had the inside track on all other scribes. His publication featured his report—some would call it a "puff piece"—on the wheelings and dealings by Hulbert and his new cronies under the headline "The Diamond Squared." The writer also uncharitably characterized famed baseball scribe Harry Chadwick as "the Old Man of the Sea . . . a dead weight on the neck of the game."

Chadwick, no stranger to journalistic skirmishes, responded in the *New York Clipper* wondering why the new National League had utilized what he called cloak-and-dagger means to achieve a moral end. "Reform should not fear the light of day," wrote Chadwick, continuing that the new league was "a sad blunder . . . a star-chamber method of attaining . . . objects." He suggested that it would have been fairer to have proffered invitations to all existing professional teams.

The *St. Louis Dispatch* questioned the morality that the operators of the new National League claimed as a cornerstone of their enterprise. The Phillies, the *Dispatch* pointed out, were not welcomed into the National League because of the record of gambling that had attached itself to that club. However, the Mutuals of New York were admitted to the new enterprise despite their record of dishonest play. The writer of the *Dispatch* article therefore concluded that the highly lucrative New York–area demographics was of greater value to the National League than the reform morality they professed.

In Chicago, Albert Goodwill Spalding, premier exponent of the underhand delivery who had pitched the Boston team to four straight pennants from 1872 to 1875 and would become Hulbert's lieutenant as player-manager of the White Stockings, told the *Tribune*: "Championship matches will draw a better average attendance. . . . The public will feel confident that strong men will meet."

The *Tribune* also reported that Spalding would open "a large emporium in Chicago where he will sell all kinds of baseball goods and turn his place into the headquarters for the Western ball clubs." Spalding's players would be garbed in uniforms from the sturdy shelves of his shop. He would produce a different colored cap for each player's position, making the team resemble, in the *Tribune's* phrase, "a Dutch bed of tulips." For Spalding, life then was a bed of roses. The new league granted him a monopoly to supply the official baseballs and a license to publish its official guide.

Life was not as fragrant an enterprise for the new National League players. Although they looked the epitome of pro baseball players in their flashy uniforms, players were almost totally controlled by the owners. They had to pay for their own uniforms. Players were also required to donate 50 cents a day each in expense money for road trips. These charges made players complain, but their protests were to no avail. Ignored by the owners, the players were attacked in some newspapers as being an overpampered lot. Fifty cents was also the admission price to National League games, although fans arriving after the third inning could gain access to the baseball doings for a dime.

Two master strokes for the new National League that set it apart from all that had gone before were control of the time and cost of the games. The ban on Sunday games excluded attendance by most lower-class laborers, for many of them even worked a half-day on

Saturdays. The relatively expensive 50-cent ticket price also controlled the type of individual who attended the games. The ban on the sale of alcohol further created a crowd profile, one that was aimed at attendance by a middle-class spectator.

That first National League season of 1876 was 30 years removed from "the first baseball game" ever played in the United States on June 19, 1846, on Elysian Field in Hoboken, New Jersey, a short ferry ride across the Hudson River. In those three decades between the first baseball game and the first National League game, a myriad of changes had taken place in the sport that would become the national pastime, and more, many more transformations were in the offing.

THREE

===

The Backdrop

*The future of baseball is without limit. The time is coming when there
will be great amphitheaters throughout the United States in which
citizens shall be able to see the teams take part in the finest athletic
struggles of the world.*
—Albert G. Spalding

BALLPARKS

The early environment of baseball games was that of a gentlemen's
affair marked by the absence of spectators except for those invited by
the teams. What spectators there were, lolled about on the grass or
sat on chairs or benches. The umpire was generally attired in tails
and a tall black top hat, and in those early years he seated himself at a
table along a baseline. Circa 1860, the general public became more
and more involved as spectators, and winning replaced gentlemanly
ways as baseball's operative factor.

FACTOID

Capitoline Grounds in Brooklyn opened May 5, 1864. A makeshift bar was always set up on one side of the field. Out in right field, there was a round brick outhouse. A player homering over that building was awarded a bottle of Champagne. Intentional flooding of the park each November 15 enabled it to be converted into an ice skating rink.

The Cincinnati Red Stockings began play in 1876 in the National League in a ballpark located in an area known as Chester Park. In order to get to the ball game, fans had to ride on special trains or in carriages. Crowds of 3,000 were common and considered a good payday for the team. When the National League came into being, the White Stockings played their home games in a rickety wooden park on Dearborn between 23rd and 24th streets on Chicago's West Side.

The St. Louis Browns (aka Perfectos—an odd name for a club with a not-so-perfect track record) left the National League twice, then returned and finished 12th twice, 11th three times, 10th once, ninth once, and fifth place once in the years 1892–1899. The owner, Christopher Von der Ahe, was nicknamed the "Millionaire Sportsman." In 1880, he purchased Sportsman's Park, which was then given a covered grandstand.

"Chris kicked like a mule about that project," wrote sportswriter J. Roy Stockton. "He argued that the fans wouldn't get as thirsty in the covered stands. But he finally compromised . . . with the understanding that there would be sizeable bleachers where the sun could get in its thirst-producing licks."

Von der Ahe was known for his promotional genius. After that original park burned in 1891, he bought a National League franchise. Always one who didn't mind taking an extra chance, making an extra buck, he installed a honky-tonk, amusement park rides, chute-the-chutes (tubs that plunged with their riders into a pool), and night horseracing. Von der Ahe gave the park a new name: "the Coney Island of the West." One of his more ingenious, some would say crass, moves was offering a 50-cent doubleheader: baseball and Buffalo Bill's Wild West Show. Yes, Sitting Bull was there. The popular tunes of the day were played by the Silver Cornet Band—an all-female aggregation bedecked in long striped skirts and elegant blouses with leg-of-mutton sleeves and broad white sailor hats.

During the 1880s and 1890s most parks were surrounded by wooden stands and a wooden fence. Some of the stands were partially protected by a roof, while others were simple wooden seats of sun-bleached boards—which is how the word "bleachers" came to be. When those parks were filled to capacity, fans were allowed to stand around the infield or take up viewing perches in the far reaches of the outfield. As late as 1900 some clubs even allowed fans to park their automobiles or carriages in the outfield. Some of the playing fields were enclosed by four-foot wooden fences to keep overly exuberant fans in their place and off the field of play. These barriers were effective and kept mobs at bay.

On May 25, 1888, the second coming of the South End Grounds in Boston was upon the world of baseball. One of the most prominent features in the only two-tiered baseball park Boston has ever known was a cathedral-like grandstand.

FACTOID

For $650 per season, concessionaires purchased the exclusive right to sell items such as fruit, tobacco, seat cushions, and other souvenirs in the Boston ballpark.

Places where games were played became marketing tools for owners seeking to sell a total experience. Carriage parking was available for a price. Ladies were offered armchairs. St. George's Grounds on Staten Island was a show in itself. "The stand is divided into two galleries and will have a seating capacity of about 5,000," was how

Sporting Life described the Staten Island baseball facility. "In the centre lower will be the ladies' refreshment parlor, and under the north end the general dining room. These unwonted attachments to a baseball stand have been added . . . to make the place a popular summer evening resort."

John B. Day transferred the Troy National League franchise to New York City in 1883; the team was then known as the New Yorkers. The other team in town, the New York Metropolitans of the fledgling American Association, also fought for fans. Both teams played their season-opening games on a field across from Central Park's northeastern corner at 110th Street and Fifth Avenue. The land on which they played was owned by *New York Herald Tribune* publisher James Gordon Bennett. The wealthy publisher and some of his society friends had played polo on that field. The baseball field came to be known as the Polo Grounds.

Charlie Bennett, a popular catcher with Detroit for eight National League seasons, lost both legs in a railway accident in 1894. Charlie Bennett's Park, or simply Bennett Park, opened in 1896. Built of wood and with a seating capacity of 5,000, it was the home field (3.3 acres) of the Detroit Tigers of the Western League, at the northwest corner of Michigan and Trumbull in the city of Detroit. Other ballparks of that time occupied larger sites, ranging from 5.7 acres (Ebbets Field in Brooklyn) to 9.6 acres (Hilltop Park in New York).

In 1897, a game between Boston and Baltimore drew more than 25,000 fans. The overflow crowd was allowed to stand just a few feet behind the infielders, creating a situation where any ball hit into the throng was ruled an automatic ground-rule double.

Philadelphia, which had been expelled from the National League in 1876 when it refused to make a final western swing, returned to the league in 1883, when successful sporting goods manufacturer Alfred A. Reach transferred the Worcester, Massachusetts, franchise to the City of Brotherly Love. The team played its games at Recreation Park, an irregular plot of land bordered by Columbia and Ridge avenues and 24th and 25th streets. However, the seating capacity of the park proved too small for the profits Reach was interested in.

On April 30, 1887, Huntington Grounds, a new Philadelphia park that seated 20,000, was opened. Distances were 335 feet in left field, 408 in center field, and 272 in right field. The outfield contained a banked bicycle track that made outfielders huff and puff a bit going uphill after fly balls. The center field section housed club offices and, interestingly enough, a swimming pool for players.

In 1899, the New York National League team, the Giants, moved to New York City plot 2106, lot 100, located between 155th and 157th streets at Eighth Avenue in upper Manhattan. The location was called "the new Polo Grounds," a horseshoe-shaped stadium with Coogan's Bluff on one side and the Harlem River on the other. Polo was never played there. The Polo Grounds seated 55,897, the most of any facility in the National League. A four-story, misshapen structure with seats close to the playing field and overhanging stands, it was an odd ballpark that afforded fans the opportunity to be close to the action. There were 4,600 bleacher seats, 2,730 field boxes, 1,084 upper boxes, 5,138 upper reserved boxes, and 2,318 general admission seats. The majority of those who came to the Polo Grounds sat in the remaining lower general admission seats. The visitors' bullpen was just a bench located in the boondocks of left center field. There was no shade from the sun for the visitors or protection from Giants fans who pelted opposing pitchers with pungent projectiles and other offensive items.

The upper left field deck hung over the lower deck; and it was virtually impossible for a fly ball to get into the lower deck because of the projection of the upper deck. The overhang triggered many arguments, for if a ball happened to graze the front of the overhang, it was a home run. The double decks in right field were even. The short distances and the asymmetrical shape of the convoluted ballpark resulted in drives rebounding off the right field and left field walls like billiard shots. Over the years, hitters and fielders on the New York Giants familiar with the pool table walls of the ballpark had a huge advantage over opposing teams.

The environment at many of those ballparks made it difficult for fans to follow the action clearly. Even though scorecards and programs were sold, no public address system existed, and there were no names or numbers on the players' uniforms.

Players were sometimes pressed into service to double as ticket takers. And during breaks in the action on the field, the dull moments were enlivened by the festive performances of brass bands.

Fires and progress would make steel and concrete replace the wood and timber of the 19th-century ballparks. The odd dimensions of stadiums, the marching bands, even the real grass in some instances—all of these would ultimately become footnotes to baseball history.

RULES

Conscious control of the style, the quality, and the substance of the game were always the primary concerns of the club owners. There was constant tinkering with rules. The owners—who preferred to be called "magnates"—overreached and overreacted. Bickering, almost for the sake of bickering, it seemed, became a cornerstone of organized baseball. Changes in rules, the disbursement of gate receipts, selection and behavior of umpires, player salaries and behavior, franchise solvency and insolvency—all of these, and more, frequently formed the subject matter of acrimonious meetings and encounters among the magnates. The most positive changes in the game were in the rules enacted that moved baseball closer in look and tone to the 20th century.

Baseball played in 1876 bore some resemblance to the game of today, but its style was very different. The baseball weighed not less than 5 ounces and no more than 5½ ounces. Its circumference was no less than 9 inches nor more than 9½ inches. Those dimensions of the baseball have remained the same throughout the history of the national pastime, but other features of the game have undergone dramatic changes.

In 1876, the pitcher (still referred to in some circles as a "bowler") stood 45 feet away from a maskless catcher and threw underhand to the plate. The more-successful pitchers depended a great deal on their ability to vary the velocity of their pitches. The catcher stood a few feet behind the batter and worked hard at catching the ball on its first bounce.

Batters had the privilege of directing hurlers to throw the ball "high" or "low." There was no formal strike zone, and nine balls constituted a walk. An "unfair" ball delivered by the hurler was a pitch not to the batter's liking. Once a batter had two strikes and allowed a third "good pitch" to go by, a warning was issued by the umpire. If the pitcher delivered a fourth "good pitch" and it was not swung at, the batter was retired on a "called strikeout." Batters were charged with a time at bat if they walked. The more-successful hitters made an art of slamming the pitched ball through the infield, and hard grounders became staples of batting success. Real gloves for fielders would not come until later.

The look of the playing field was a major concern of the rules makers in 1877. Home plate was moved from its position just back of the edge of the diamond to a spot exactly within the diamond or square, the location it occupies today. Rules were also instituted that mandated a 15-inch-square canvas-covered base as standard.

In 1879, pitchers enjoyed their final season of being allowed to serve up nine balls before a batter was awarded first base on a walk. By 1882, seven balls meant a walk. And in 1889, the present regulation of four balls constituting a walk came into being and became the standard for professional baseball. That season of 1879, the rule that declared a runner out if he was hit by a batted ball was also adopted. It was a much-needed regulation, eliminating the practice of base runners' running into a ball to prevent infielders from making a play.

In 1880, hurlers moved five feet farther from the batters when the pitching distance to home plate was changed from 45 feet to 50 feet. That same year the National League owners announced that players could be barred "from play and from pay" for "insubordination or misconduct of any kind."

Albert Spalding in 1882 made his Chicago players sign a pledge that they would totally abstain from the consumption of whiskey, wine, and beer. Spalding brooked no nonsense. Enforcement of the pledge came in the form of a private detective who was hired to snoop on players.

Pitchers were emancipated in 1884 when all restrictions on their windups were removed. Now hurlers were free to use any type of motion they desired, just as long as they faced the batter at the moment of their windup. In 1885, batters were permitted to use bats with one flat side and paddle at the ball. Pitchers that season were credited with an assist on a batter's strikeout.

Several of the changes in rules and innovations developed by teams attempted to speed up the game and reduce unruly behavior. By the mid-1880s, fixed coaching lines were in place. In theory, coaches were now restricted to plying their trade from a designated area and not running up and down in a helter-skelter manner, venting their opinions. The fixed coaching lines helped a bit, but many of the coaches still strayed about at will.

In 1886, the game was speeded up a bit more when the five-minute "lost ball" rule was dropped. Umpires were now allowed to replace a lost ball instantaneously rather than follow the previous practice of allowing players five minutes to forage for a lost ball before a new ball was put into play.

The season of 1886 witnessed some intriguing new rules. The captain of the home team was allowed to decide which team batted first. The pitcher's box was enlarged from 6 × 4 feet to 7 × 4 feet. And the troublesome rule that credited a runner with a stolen base for each base he advanced on another player's hit came into being. Not until 1898 was the present stolen base rule put into effect.

Experimentation and also some lasting changes marked the 1887 season. For that year only, four strikes were allowed a batter—the initial called third strike did not count—and walks were counted in the batting average of a player as hits. A batter was also allowed to take first base when struck by a pitch—a rule that has lasted until the present day. Pitchers in 1887 were banned for all time from taking a run and a jump before delivering the ball. And batters lost for all time their privilege of demanding a "high" or a "low" pitch. From 1887 on they had to go for what was served up.

Not all the rules promulgated, however, added to the forward movement of the game. The 1887 rules counting a walk as a hit and allowing batters four strikes put the hitters on parade. A dozen of them batted over .400 that 1894 season. Recomputation today of those averages, taking away the "walk hits," leaves only three hitters with averages over .400. Harry Stovey, a .402 batter, recomputed, drops to .286. Tip O'Neill of the American Association St. Louis Browns batted a glittering .492 and was the league leader in runs, doubles, triples, and homers. Tip didn't walk a lot and his recomputed batting average is still a lofty .442.

In 1888, the three-strike rule was restored and a walk was no longer credited in a player's batting average as a hit or a time at bat. Thus, the game moved even closer to the rules of today. However, a revisionist step also was enacted that year, crediting a batter with a hit when his batted ball hit a base runner. That 1888 season also saw the enactment of a rule that a ball hit over the fence in fair territory was a ground-rule double and not a home run if the fence was less than 210 feet from home plate.

FACTOID

Rules for walks and strikeouts varied from season to season, with the ball count going as high as nine in 1874. By 1889, four balls were needed for a walk, and three strikes for a strikeout.

Balls and strikes in 1889 moved closer to the standard pattern that has persisted to this day when a rule mandated that four balls equal a walk. Other changes that year included no error charged to the catcher on a passed ball, and no error assigned to a pitcher for a walk, wild pitch, balk, or hit batter. The sacrifice bunt was also recognized, but the batter executing it was charged with a time at bat.

Prior to 1891, substitutions were allowed in a game only when a player was injured or when permission was granted by the opposing team. That 1891 season the lasting pattern for substitution came into being: substitution was now allowed at any time during a game.

In 1893, a misreading of a diagram set the pitching distance from the mound—where a rubber slab 12 inches long and 4 inches wide was now mandatory—to home plate at 60 feet 6 inches. Actually, the rules makers had changed the distance from 50 feet to 60 feet, but the surveyor read 60 feet as 60' 6". And that is how the distance has remained to this time. Another rule mandated that all bats be completely round. That 1893 season the rule came into being that a sacrifice would not be counted as a time at bat for a hitter.

From 1894 to the end of the century, still more rule refinements made the game of baseball more closely approximate in style and substance what it is today. Some of the major changes in rules in those years included:

- Attempted bunts that went foul were ruled strikes.
- The infield fly rule was introduced.
- A foul tip was a strike.
- The maximum diameter of a bat was increased from 2½ inches to 2¾ inches.
- Errors were not charged to infielders attempting to complete a double play unless throws were so errant that runners were able to gain an extra base, and catchers were not charged with errors when attempting to prevent a stolen base unless they threw so wildly that runners were able to gain an additional base.
- The balk rule was adopted.
- Batters were allowed to run past first base without being tagged out after returning to the bag.
- The present-day five-sided plate was introduced.

UMPIRES

Mother, may I slug the umpire
May I slug him right away?
So he cannot be here, Mother,
When the clubs begin to play?

Let me clasp his throat, dear mother,
In a dear delightful grip
With one hand and with the other
Bat him several in the lip.

Let me climb his frame, dear mother,
While the happy people shout;
I'll not kill him, dearest mother,
I will only knock him out.

Let me mop the ground up, Mother,
With his person, dearest do;
If the ground can stand it, Mother,
I don't see why you can't, too.

Mother, may I slug the umpire,
Slug him right between the eyes?
If you let me do it, Mother,
You shall have the champion prize

—Untitled (*Slug the Umpire*) by Anonymous,
Chicago Tribune, 1886

Early umpires were selected from the assembled crowd or even from the ranks of players. They personified the amateur spirit of the game of baseball. And since it was an "honor" to be called to that task, the early umpires received no financial compensation for their duties. They wore whatever clothing they wished. Some of the more stylish early fellows showed up bedecked in Prince Albert coat, cane, and top hat. They sat at a table or took up a stance or kneeled on a stool a brave distance from home plate along the first-base line.

In 1876, Philadelphia's William McLean became the first professional umpire when he umpired the first game in National League history between Boston and Philadelphia on April 22. On August 6, 1877, there was a bit of an umpire problem that got a lot of attention. The National League rule specified that the home team submit three names of approved local men as a possible umpires for each game. The visiting team was allowed the choosing of one of them at random. In Louisville, Chicago's Cal McVey plucked out a slip with name of Devinney on it. Then an annoyed McVey grabbed the hat and discovered all three slips had Devinney's name. The White Stockings demanded someone else (not named Devinney) to umpire. The game was played, and Chicago ended Louisville's six-game winning streak.

The National League in 1878 revolutionized things a bit by ruling that umpires would be paid $5 a game and gave the arbiters the right to fine players up to $20 for the use of foul language. Umps were also given the power to eject rowdy fans.

FACTOID

On April 4, 1879, the Providence Grays began to sell 15-cent tickets for a section in center field called the "bull pen." Admission at that price could be purchased only starting during the fifth inning. The section sold out daily.

In 1879, the National League named 20 men whom it deemed fit to be a cadre of umpires. For the sake of logistical convenience, the umpires chosen all lived in or close to cities where National League franchises were located. Prior to 1879, rival captains of teams had mutually agreed on whom they preferred to umpire a game. Now the league ruled that umpires could be chosen only from the select list of 20 men. These umpires were given the authority to impose fines for illegal acts.

In 1882, National League umpire Richard Higham became the only major league umpire ever expelled from the game after the league judged him guilty of collusion with gamblers.

The gradually increased duties and independence of umpires were reflected in an 1882 ruling that abolished the practice of arbiters appealing to fans and players for guidance on a disputed play. Now umps were on their own to "call them as they saw them." And from 1882 on, all players except for the team captains were theoretically banned from engaging in any kind of menacing or meaningless banter with the umpire.

That 1882 season the American Association put in place a salaried staff of three umpires to be paid $140 a month. It was also the American Association that innovated clothing umps in blue caps and coats—a uniform that was aimed at giving the arbiters an air of authority and respectability, one that would set them off from the crowd. Those uniforms were to become part of the folklore of the game, the dress code for the "men in blue."

In 1883, the National League copied the practice of the American Association, appointing four umpires for the season who drew salaries of $1,000 each. To ensure neutrality, to quell complaints that the new arbiters would not be political appointees, all the umpires were unknowns who came from cities that did not have National League franchises. The four men operated under trying conditions— serving without tenure, at the suffrage of the owners. Complaints by any four teams were grounds for the firing of any of the umpires. It was no surprise when just one of the four umpires made it through the entire season.

Changing rules, polemics in sports sections of newspapers criticizing umpires, the rugged nature of play—all of these made the work of the men in blue a tough task. Such terms as "daylight crime," "robbery," and "home umpire" were part of the lexicon of the times applied to the alleged foibles and flaws of arbiters.

In 1884, barbed wire was fastened around the field in Baltimore to contain the fans. That same season an umpire was beaten by an angry mob when he called a game a tie because of darkness. Police escorts were commonplace to move umpires out of ballparks and away from the menace of irate fans.

Dumping on the umpire was a practice encouraged by owners, who realized that fans howled in delight at the sight of authority being humiliated. "Fans who despise umpires," Albert Spalding noted, "are simply showing their democratic right to protest against tyranny." The protests pushed profits at the box office, and owners willingly paid fines meted out to players by umpires.

The system of two umpires working a game was instituted in 1887 in postseason competition between the National League and the American Association. The first set of double officials was John Gaffney and John Kelley.

As a class, those early arbiters were a colorful and tenacious group of men—they had to be, considering the not-so-genteel band of athletes they had to deal with. Umpire Billy McLean, who plied his trade in Boston and Providence, was a quick-triggered type. An ex-boxer, McLean kept himself in top physical condition; it was reported that he once arose at 4 A.M. and walked from his home in Boston to his umpiring job in Providence. It was not reported how he got back to Boston.

John Gaffney was called the "King of Umpires" because of his longevity and resiliency. At one point, Gaffney was the highest-paid umpire, earning a salary of $2,500 plus expenses. Bob Ferguson was another standout man in blue. "Umpiring always came as easy to me," he said, "as sleeping on a featherbed. Never change a decision, never stop to talk to a man. Make 'em play ball and keep their mouths shut, and never fear but the people will be on your side and you'll be called the king of umpires."

Tim Hurst, who coined the now-famous phrase about umpires, "The pay is good, and you can't beat the hours—three to five," was another of the fabled arbiters of 19th-century baseball. A rather smallish man who came out of the coal mining region of Pennsylvania, Hurst was quick witted and quick fisted. In 1897, during the course of a game in Cincinnati, Hurst was struck in the face by a stein of beer that was hurled out of the stands. Hurst flung the stein back; it hit a spectator and knocked him out. A frenzied mob surged out onto the field heading for Hurst. Policemen made contact with the umpire first. They charged him with assault and battery and arrested the irate Hurst, who was fined $100 and court costs by a judge.

Then there was the fracas in Washington in which Hurst mixed it up verbally with Pittsburgh's Pink Hawley, Jake Stenzel, and Denny Lyons. The quartet agreed to meet after the game to settle things once and for all. Hurst, who always had a sensational sense of timing, went to work quickly. He punched Hawley in the face, smashed his foot into the shins of Lyons, and roughed up Stenzel.

"Timothy, what is all the excitement?" asked National League President Nick Young, who as it turned out just happened to be passing by.

"Somebody dropped a dollar bill, Uncle Nick," replied Hurst, "and I said it was mine."

"Oh, you're sure that's all?" asked Young. "It looked to me like there was some kind of a riot going on. Did the dollar bill really belong to you?"

"Not really. It belonged to Hawley, but these other two tried their best to take it away from him, and I wouldn't let them. It was just pink tea."

"Timothy, you did the right thing." Young smiled. "Now let's leave these follows alone. Come and take a walk with me."

Two umpires from that epoch went on to become National League presidents—John Heyder and Tom Lynch. Both men confessed to recurring nightmares of their time as umpires.

With all the pain and the abuse of the job of umpiring, there were some redeeming aspects. The early umpires loved the game of baseball. They earned an average salary of $1,500 for seven months of employment, and as Hurst noted, it was a job where "you can't beat the hours. "

In 1898, the Brush Resolution was passed, slightly improving the umpire's lot. John T. Brush, National League mogul, pushed owners into endorsing a 21-point program to do away with the bullying of umpires. Expulsion for "villainously foul language" and umpire baiting were at the heart of the resolution.

The "purification plan" never worked and was ultimately given up as hopeless—no case ever reached the appointed discipline board, but it did raise the consciousness of the public, players, and writers about the plight of umpires forced to contend with the riotous behavior of scrappy and excitable players.

"Kill the umpire" would be a phrase of symbolic import in the future and that was a large step forward, for in the not-so-genteel days of the gilded age, that phrase had a darker and more sinister meaning. A graphic example took place in New York City in 1860. An umpire's decision led to a riot in which the visiting team was driven from the field in a hail of stones. The umpire fled for his life.

WOMEN

Almost from the start, women were part of the baseball scene. At picnics and social gatherings, with friends and family, women in full Victorian dress played the game, running the bases, fielding ground balls, taking their turns at bat.

It was felt that the rowdiness of the sport—fights among fans, catcalling, and throwing objects, even violence toward players and umpires—would be lessened in the presence of women. Teams set up tents and refreshments for female fans. Admission was often free of charge to local games. Ladies Day, a late 19th-century promotion, came into being. It was designed to attract women fans to baseball, help increase attendance, and quell the fervor of the sometimes unruly crowds.

There were women who opted for the right to play the game under organized conditions. Vassar College, seeking more exercise outlets for women, formed recreational teams in the 1860s. Soon other colleges did the same. None of these teams lasted, however, because these colleges bowed to the pressures of disapproving mothers. In 1880, women at Smith College attempted to establish baseball teams. The same negativity to the idea resurfaced.

But women's touring teams did attract a following. Showmen with an entrepreneurial feel organized women's teams to serve as barnstorming novelty acts across America. The Springfield (Illinois) Blondes and Brunettes was reportedly the first team out there. But sadly it went out of business after four games. The sexism of the day was on display and doomed the Springfield team with comments like "a revolting exhibition of impropriety." Promoters in Philadelphia fielded two teams in 1883—the Red Stockings and the Blue Stockings. Free admission and the novelty of it all drew more than 500 women spectators for a match in Camden, New Jersey.

By the 1890s, women's' teams, sometimes described as "bloomer girls," were popular. One Reading, Pennsylvania, men's team even fielded a woman pitcher to boost attendance. Even though she pitched only part of the ninth inning, the local paper commented, "For a woman, she is a success."

Overall, though, prejudice against women participating in organized baseball was a nasty part of the cultural milieu. On March 12, 1892, a bill before the New York State Assembly was put forward "to prohibit the employment of females as baseball players."

UNIFORMS AND EQUIPMENT

> We used no mattress on our hands,
> No cage upon our face;
> We stood right up and caught the ball
> With courage and with grace.
>
> —George Ellard, catcher

Uniforms

The first "uniform," an outfit modeled after that of cricket players, was introduced by the Knickerbocker Baseball Club in 1851. The Knickerbockers wore straw hats, long blue woolen trousers, and white flannel shirts. Webbed belts held the entire uniform and the image together. By 1855, the straw hats were no longer on the scene now replaced by flat-topped mohair caps, also standard cricket equipment.

In 1868, the Cincinnati Red Stockings introduced knee-length knickerbocker pants. Although the shortened pants spurred jeers from players and fans, the garment caught on, and today's baseball pants are in length modeled after them. The Red Stockings used cricket flannel and, to keep costs down, uniforms were ordered in just three basic sizes, so that a player could substitute for a worn-out uniform part quickly and economically.

A flashiness characterized those early uniformed teams, as exemplified by the 1871 Athletics and the 1876 Louisville club. The Athletics were all the rage in white shirts and pants, blue caps and stockings. In 1876 Louisville players were a vision in white uniforms and caps, blue stockings, a two-toned belt, and across their shirt fronts in navy blue in big letters the word "Louisville."

A more sedate look came to National League uniforms in 1878. As recommended by the *Official Baseball Guide*, the uniform was white and only one other color. In the view of the *Guide*, that was the "prettiest" combination. The White Stockings of Chicago sported a different-colored cap according to a player's position. A. G. Spalding figured it would be easier for fans to pick out the players, and he also thought the different-colored haberdashery lent a touch of style to his team.

All types of unusual, some would say outlandish, uniforms existed prior to 1882. That season, the National League ruled that teams would no longer be allowed free choice in baseball fashion. White was mandated for belts, pants, and ties. Shirts and caps were restricted to the use of designated colors: Boston, red; Cleveland, navy blue; Chicago, white; Providence, light blue; Buffalo, gray; Troy, green; Detroit, old gold; Worcester, brown.

By 1883, regulations for uniforms were rescinded and applied only to the color of the lightweight silk stockings that were all the vogue. Oddly, when the 1899 season began, maroon stockings were worn by the Chicago White Stockings. That season, owner Chris Von der Ahe changed his team's uniforms around in his zest for more color—the new garments featured red trim and red-striped stockings. The new uniforms brought new nicknames for the St. Louis team—Cardinals or Redbirds, they were called, and so they would remain.

By the 1890s the quilted knickers of the decade before had been replaced by most teams who now wore comfortable uniforms made of flannel adorned with separate sliding pads. The total cost of these more "modern" uniforms was an expensive, for that time, $56.

One of the more arresting, some would say funereal-looking, uniforms of 19th-century players was that worn by the New York Giants. Designed and sold to the team by pitcher Tim Keefe, the tight-fitting uniform was all black except for "New York" spelled out in white raised letters across the chest.

An altercation between Cap Anson and King Kelly revolution-ized the style of belt loops. Kelly once snared Anson by his belt loop, preventing him from making a throw. Anson was so frustrated and angered by the incident that he prevailed on a sporting-goods maker to thread the belt through a pants' fabric and thus reduce the avail-able surface an opponent could pull on.

As the 19th century gave way to the 20th, numbers appeared on the backs of the uniforms of baseball players—an accommodation not to television or radio (that would come later), but to those busi-ness types who produced scorecards and wished to sell them to fans who could use them more pleasurably by being able to pick out the number of a player easily and thus keep a more accurate score.

Baseball shoes have undergone dramatic changes through the passing seasons. In 1877 the Harvard team replaced canvas shoes with leather ones that were laced around the ankles. More and more, high topped shoes gave way to lower-cut ones designed to enhance a runner's speed. Spikes were in wide use by the late 1880s and proved effective as an aid to a player's speed and traction. Spikes also served another purpose—terror.

"Give 'em steel" was the battle cry of Cleveland Spider manager Patsy Tebeau in the 1890s, "and plenty of it." The Spiders heeded Tebeau's advice and spent hours sharpening and filing their spikes. They were not much as ballplayers, but the Spiders did terrorize the opposition for a time with their razor-sharp spikes.

In 1890, heel and toe plates, once sold individually, were collectively attached to the bottom of low-cut baseball shoes to enhance and improve a player's grip and traction.

By 1900, the look of the game, the style and the feel of uniforms had undergone radical changes in just a few short decades. And although the game of baseball would remain more or less the same, uniforms would be altered, adjusted, refined still more in the years of the 20th century.

Gloves

The evolution of baseball also saw a revolution in the style and substance of playing equipment and uniforms. The day of purposeful and also cosmetic equipment, like the sweatband, headband, batting tee, and batting glove, was far off in the future, but all equipment and uniforms have roots stretching back to the 19th century.

Bumps, bruises, and fractured fingers were part of the lot of baseball players for many of those years. The game was rough and tumble, the players were macho and manly, and any type of protective garb was frowned upon.

Then one day in 1875, in a game against Boston, outfielder Charlie Waite of New Haven sauntered onto the field to play first base, his left hand adorned with an ordinary leather dress glove. The garment was an inconspicuous flesh color; Waite sought to attract as little attention as possible and did not wish to be considered less than manly by the partisans in the stands and his peers on the field.

Waite was able to glove his hand but unable to cover up what he was doing. The pioneer's "sissified" approach—the protective garment on his hand—triggered taunts and jeers from fans and players. Nevertheless, Waite played on, protected, swapping the pain of ridicule for the pain of a batted baseball.

One who always appreciated an idea whose time had come was Albert Spalding, a man who also knew too well the pain of a hard ball on bare hand or bone. A year after Waite's glove appeared, Spalding and his brothers launched his sporting goods business, a staple of which was the production of baseball gloves. And in 1877, when A. G. shifted from pitching to playing first base, he also shifted to wearing a glove.

"When I'd recalled that every ball pitched had to be returned, and that every hit one coming my way from fielders, outfielders, or hot from the bat must be caught and stopped, some idea may be gained of the punishment received," noted Spalding in defense of his wearing a glove.

The glove Spalding wore was padded but not disguised in flesh color like Waite's; it was dark leather and there for all to see. Years later when he was no longer actively playing the game, Albert Spalding mused on his early baseball glove experiences:

> The first glove I ever saw on the hand of a ball player in a game was worn by Charles C. Waite, in Boston, in 1875. He had come from New Haven and was playing at first base. The glove worn by him was of flesh color, with a large, round opening in the back. Now, I had for a good while felt the need of some sort of hand protection for myself. For several years I had pitched in every game played by the Boston team, and had developed severe bruises on the inside of my left hand.
>
> Therefore, I asked Waite about his glove. He confessed that he was a bit ashamed to wear it, but had it on to save his hand. He also admitted that he had chosen a color as inconspicuous as possible, because he didn't care to attract attention. He added that the opening on the back was for purpose of ventilation.
>
> Meanwhile my own hand continued to take its medicine with utmost regularity, occasionally being bored with a warm twister that hurt excruciatingly. Still, it was not until 1877 that I overcame

my scruples against joining the "kid-glove aristocracy" by donning a glove. When I did at last decide to do so, I did not select a flesh-colored glove, but got a black one, and cut out as much of the back as possible to let the air in.

Happily, in my case, the presence of a glove did not call out the ridicule that had greeted Waite. I had been playing so long and had become so well known that the innovation seemed rather to evoke sympathy than hilarity. I found that the glove, thin as it was, helped considerably, and inserted one pad after another until a good deal of relief was afforded. If anyone wore a padded glove before this date I do not know it. The "pillow mitt" was a later innovation.

Spalding was the trendsetter, and gloves began to catch on in all types of variations. Catcher Henry Fabian of New Orleans in 1880 utilized two gloves on his left hand and placed a piece of sheet lead between the surfaces. Cap Anson sported kid gloves with cut-off fingertips on his throwing hand. Anson's catcher, Frank "Old Silver" Flint, got by with thin leather gloves cushioned with raw beefsteak.

By 1886, finger gloves were in fairly widespread use, and instead of two gloves most players now used only one. By the 1890s, gloves were standard equipment in baseball. A few players, like Fred Dunlap, however, went through their entire careers without ever using a glove. Dunlap claimed he didn't need "the thing," and maybe he was right. He led the National League four years in fielding in the 1880s sans glove.

And there were others who, like Dunlap, could not give up the old bare-handed ways. "The game of baseball is being spoiled by allowing players to wear these abominations known as mitts," said Boston's Harry Schafer. "Players do not have to show skill in handling balls with those mitts in their hands. Those who cannot play without them should get out of the game and give way to those who can."

One player who benefited greatly from the use of a glove was Lave Cross, a massive catcher. Converted in 1892 to a third baseman when he joined Philadelphia, Cross played the hot corner buttressed by his catcher's mitt. Using his oversized glove like a flyswatter, Cross smacked down and snared virtually every ball hit his way. "They're playing infield with barn doors," some reporters complained.

In 1895, the rules committee came up with restrictions on "barn doors." All gloves except for catchers' and first basemen's were limited to no more than 10 ounces in weight and no more than 14 inches in circumference, as measured around the palm. The smaller glove was the end of the line for a few players, like Cross, now unable just to hack away at fielding their position.

Catchers' Equipment

Actually the mouth protector, not the glove, was baseball's first bit of protective equipment. Sported by Cincinnati Reds shortstop George Wright in the 1860s, it was a patented piece of equipment and a welcome replacement for the broad rubber bands that had previously been worn around the mouth by catchers to save their teeth. Wright's sporting goods company patented, manufactured, and enjoyed some big-money days selling the mouth protector for a time, until it became a footnote to baseball history when it was replaced by the catcher's mask.

As the story goes, the captain of the Harvard team, F. Winthrop Thayer, invented the mask, using the one employed in fencing as a prototype. He then presented the new model to his catcher, James Alexander Tyny, who had issued threats of quitting the game because of fear of disfiguring his face. Not until 1877 did professional catchers adopt the mask that fans referred to as a "bird cage" and that sportswriters ridiculed with such diatribes as: "There is a good deal of beastly humbug in contrivances to protect men from things that don't happen. There is about as much sense in putting a lightning rod on a catcher as a mask."

Despite the criticisms, sales of catcher's masks became a good business. Peck and Snyder's sporting goods stores sold them for three dollars each. The store's ad copy claimed that "some of the top catchers of 1877" were using the equipment "made of wire and cushioned with soft leather . . . filled with best curled hair. They are light and easy to adjust."

FACTOID

Peck and Snyder of New York City advertised "new styles of baseball uniforms and outfits; baseball caps, eight corners with star in top of corded seams for $10 per dozen ($1 sample by mail); uniform flannel for $8 a dozen, and second quality flannels at $6 a dozen." There were also belts for 60 cents each, heavy English all-worsted hose in either solids or stripes for $2.50 each or $27 for a dozen. With cotton feet, the hose were just $24 a dozen—three dollars less for leggings.

A patent dispute between Thayer & Wright and A. G. Spalding & Brothers was on the court schedule in Chicago on February 5, 1886. In the final settlement, the claim of Thayer was upheld. He would receive a royalty on masks sold from Spalding's company. And Spalding's pathway would be laid out—the buying out of many rivals as he and his company established a sporting goods business monopoly.

The history of Albert Goodwill Spalding as entrepreneur is fascinating reading. Just after the start of the 1887 season, he stopped pitching and opened a sporting goods business, with the help of an $800 loan from his mother. At first Spalding was all about manufacturing baseballs; he paid the National League to use his balls. Then he was able to advertise them as the "official" league ball. Soon, his firm was manufacturing golf clubs, tennis racquets, basketballs, all and everything in some way connected to sport.

Spalding commented: "Americans are evoluting into a fresh-air people. They are being converted to the gospel of exercise."

> "Next to Abraham Lincoln and George Washington, the name of A. G. Spalding is the most famous in American literature. It has been blazing forth on the cover of guides to all sorts of sports, upon bats and gloves . . . for many years. Young America gets its knowledge of the past in the world of athletics from something that has 'Spalding' on it in big black letters, and for that reason, as much as any other, he is one of the national figures of our times."
>
> —*Boston Herald*

The real impetus making the catcher's mask an important part of the equipment of the national pastime took place in 1879, when the rules committee outlawed the foul-bound catch, banning catchers from retiring a batter on a foul tip caught on the first bounce. This change in rules made catchers play closer to the plate—increasing their chances of injury and increasing the need for protection.

More protection also came with the introduction of the chest protector, invented by a Hartford man as a way to eliminate the kayos of catchers who were laid low by foul balls pounding into their chest. Dubbed a sheepskin, the chest protector was placed under the uniform, but its bulging nature served as a magnet for boos. The first chest protector was reportedly employed by catcher John T. Clements of the Philadelphia Keystones in 1884.

Bats

Baseball bats throughout history have possessed an almost mystical quality. Cap Anson allegedly hung bats like hams from the ceiling in the cellar of his house, and at peak times the old baseballer had at least 500 pieces of favorite lumber seasoning away. Always on the prowl for a good piece of wood, Anson would go after ancient logs, shafts from carts, fence posts, anything he thought he could shape into good material for a baseball bat.

One of the more macabre stories about a baseball bat concerns a player named Perring, who, when the Ohio State Penitentiary was dismantled in 1880, collected the hickory wood that had formed the scaffolding and had outlived its usefulness. Perring fashioned the highly seasoned and strong wood into a bat that endured for the next two decades.

What would go down in legend as the famed Louisville Slugger, as the story goes, made its debut in 1884. Peter Browning, one of the premier batsmen of his time, broke his bat while performing for the Louisville baseball team. Faced with the pressure of a crucial game the following day, Browning prevailed on J. F. Hillerich at the local wood-turning shop to create another bat exactly like the one that had been broken. The day of the big game arrived. Hillerich had followed orders to the letter and presented Browning with a bat fashioned from the wood of a wagon tongue. Browning batted out four hits with that piece of lumber, and Hillerich and Bradsby evolved into the leading manufacturer of the baseball bat—including the famed Louisville Slugger.

Balls

The baseball stems from the most primitive of beginnings. Albert Spalding—who delighted in the fact that on May 17, 1877, his baseball was officially adopted for major league use because it was "more lively" than the early "lemon peel ball" still being used—mused about his early experiences:

> The ball was not what would be called a National League ball, nowadays, but it served every purpose. It was usually made on the spot by some boy offering up his woolen socks as an oblation, and these were raveled and wound round a bullet, a handful of strips cut from a rubber overshoe, a piece of cork or almost anything, or nothing, when anything was not available. The winding of this ball was an art, and whoever could excel in this art was looked upon as a superior being. The ball must be a perfect sphere and the threads

as regularly laid as the wire on a helix of a magnetic armature. When the winding was complete the surface of the ball was thoroughly sewed with a large needle and thread to prevent it from unwinding when a thread was cut.

The very early baseballs had personalities all their own. Their weights varied quite a bit—and a few of them barely tipped the scales at 3 ounces. Stitching sometimes consisted of crescent-shaped sections.

The covers of all the balls were made of horsehide—an aspect of the ball that remained constant until 1973. Regulation and quality control, however, was an absent item as teams "ordered up" or "doctored up" balls to meet their own needs. The better fielding clubs utilized a soft ball, while those teams who had good hitters made sure the ball they used was hard and lively.

A baseball went through a great deal of heavy duty in those early years, unlike today, when it is routinely replaced for the slightest blemish. An outstanding example of the use and overuse of a baseball took place on August 7, 1882. The Cleveland Spiders and the New York Metropolitans played out their game in the rain at the Polo Grounds in New York City. The ball that was in use from the first pitch of the game was wet, soggy, and dirty. The ninth inning was under way and the captain of the Mets asked the umpire for a new ball to replace the virtually unusable and lopsided sphere. "I can't do it," said the umpire. "You'll have to play on with what you have."

The arbiter's ruling was in the negative because the rules stated that a new ball could not be put in play except at the beginning of an inning. The ninth had begun.

That was the backdrop!

FOUR

The National League and Its Competitors

Rowdyism by the players on the field, syndicalism among the club owners, poor umpiring and talk of rival organizations . . . are the principal causes for baseball's decline.
—*New York Times*

The Grand Central Hotel
No sun,
Now rubble,
The collected debris of memories
Echoes
An anguished ring through the corridors of Manhattan
Canyons:
Where are we going?
From where
To where
Do we step?
December . . . a month . . . a day . . . a time
logged on the fresh pages of history . . .
the first and only real entry . . . a league

(*continues*)

(*continued*)

. . . a new league . . . a microscopic legion of
men bearing witness to the birth,
unfurling its colors on an industrial land to detract
from the former failure . . .
The National Association is dead,
Long live the National League!
From rubble to rubble,
From dust to dust,
New fortresses
Stretch their fledgling arms
And puncture the sky
With abbreviated zeal.
Like so many transients
Awaiting a derailed train,
The others come
And never go.
The American Association is dead
The Union Association is dead
The Players League is dead.
All gone,
All dead,
Long live the National League!

—Anonymous

THE NATIONAL LEAGUE'S FIRST SEASON, 1876

The original eight National League franchises were Chicago, managed by Al Spalding; St. Louis, led by Herman Dehlman; Hartford, piloted by Bob Ferguson; Louisville, skippered by Chick Fulmer;

Philadelphia, handled by Al Wright; Cincinnati, led by Charlie Gould; Boston, managed by Harry Wright; and New York, piloted by Bill Cammeyer.

The first game in the history of the National League took place on April 22, 1876. Boston opposed Philadelphia. Little note was taken of the event by journalists; a few lines in fine print were published in Philadelphia newspapers:

> The championship season of 1876 was opened on Saturday afternoon by the Boston and Athletic [*sic*], on the grounds of Twenty-fifth and Jefferson streets. As was anticipated there was a large turnout to witness the game, which was well worth seeing, both nines being in full force. The first inning was a blank for both clubs, although O'Rourke for the Boston and Fisler and Meyerle for the Athletic made clean hits, the latter's being a two-baser.
>
> The Athletics should have won the game but their fielding was poor. Sutton, at third, was particularly miserable, and had to be transferred. The batting of the home nine, however, was superior to that of Boston. Great interest was manifested in the event as it was really the first game of importance of the season.
> Boston . . . . 0 1 2 0 1 0 0 0 2—6
> Athletics . . . 0 1 0 0 0 3 0 0 1—5
> Runs earned—Boston, Athletics, 2. First base on errors—Boston, 6. Athletics, 3. Bases on called balls—Boston, 2. Athletics, 1. Double plays—Eggler and Coons; Force, Fouser, and Fisler. Time of game—2 hours, 45 minutes.

The first batter in the history of the National League was George Wright. Designated as the leadoff batter for Boston by his brother Harry, George became a footnote to baseball history when he was retired on a ground ball to shortstop. "Orator Jim" O'Rourke of Boston recorded the first hit in National League history.

The winning pitcher in the first National League game was Joe Borden. Then, strangely, the 22-year-old Borden, possessor of a 12–12 record, was dropped by Boston before the season was concluded. He hung on and completed the season working as a groundskeeper for Boston, but he never again pitched in a National League game.

On Monday, April 24, 1876, Boston and Philadelphia played the second game of their series, and surprisingly the press gave that contest much more recognition. The account of the game was under the heading "Baseball," and a box score and the name of the umpire were included in the reportage:

> The "Boston and Athletic Clubs" played their second game at 25th and Jefferson Streets that afternoon in the presence of about 2,000 people. The weather was disagreeable for ball playing and the spectators, wrapped up in overcoats, resorted to outbursts of applause at frequent intervals to keep their blood above the freezing point.

The Athletics, losing the toss, went to bat first, and from the start to the close of the game, outbatted and outfielded their opponents. Josephs, the pitcher of the Boston nine, was hit with ease, while the Red Stockings were unsuccessful in mastering Knight's delivery.

As a consequence of the crippled condition of Sutton's right arm, a change was made in the positions of the field of the Philadelphia nine: Sutton playing first base, Fisler at second base, and Meyerle at third base. Morrill was substituted for Parks on the Boston nine.

Staggered home starts were another feature of that first National League season. Big league baseball began in St. Louis on May 5, 1876, at the Grand Avenue Grounds, before an estimated crowd of 3,000. An account of that event reported:

> The newly formed National League of Professional Baseball Clubs played its first game in this city today when the local St. Louis entry engaged the Chicago nine. The efforts of the local team were rewarded with a 1–0 victory. Bradley, the St. Louis pitcher, gave up two hits and also made two of the seven hits St. Louis collected against the Chicago pitcher, Spalding.

George Washington Bradley would pitch the first no-hitter in National League history against Hartford on July 15 and wind up the season with a 45–19 record. The day of the four- or five-man rotation and the relief pitcher belonged to the future. Back then hurlers pitched almost all of their team's games.

That loss to St. Louis by Spalding and Chicago was just one of a meager total of 14 in 1876 for the White Stockings, who won 52 games. Many of the victories were by shutouts, and being "Chicagoed" or "whitewashed" became synonyms for a no-runs-scored loss to the White Stockings.

FACTOID

Teams carried few substitutes in the early days. Some teams only had 10 or 12 players. When Indianapolis played 114 games in the 1876 season, they had only one pitcher and one catcher, both of whom played every game.

Rolling past most of their opposition, the Windy City team won the first pennant in National League history. Spalding dazzled and befuddled hitters, winning 47 games to lead the league.

"On receiving the ball," a writer for the *New York Star* wrote about Spalding, "he raises it in both hands until it is on a level with his left eye. Striking an attitude he gazes at it two or three minutes in a contemplative way, and then turns it around once or twice to be sure that it is not an orange or coconut. Assured that he had the genuine article . . . . [and] after a scowl at the shortstop, and a glance at home plate, [he] finally delivers the ball with the precision and rapidity of a cannon shot."

Eastern team "escapees" Cap Anson, Deacon White, Ross Barnes, and Cal McVey also made major contributions to the efforts of the White Stockings. Barnes, capitalizing on the "fair-foul" hit (all a ball had to do at that time was be in fair territory for any part of its trajectory), batted a league-leading .429. First baseman McVey recorded a .347 average and also won five of the six games he pitched when Al Spalding, manager and super hurler, decided to rest his arm and play a little first base.

Chicago scored 88 runs in a span of four straight games in July, setting a record that has never been topped, although it was a mark set when fielders went bare-handed after a ball. And on September 26, 1876, Chicago clinched the first pennant in National League history by trimming Hartford 7–6.

"They won," declared the *Chicago Tribune*, "and now, despite every combination, every abuse, every unfairness, they have played themselves fairly to the front, and so cleanly that nothing can throw off the grip they have on the flag."

Hartford did win nine games in a row near the end of the season, but it was too small a winning streak, too late in the chase. Once again the *Chicago Tribune* served up lavish praise for the hometown team, lauding "Captain Spalding" for the heroic efforts that made the White Stockings work efficiently as a team while denigrating others, to whom the newspaper referred as "some gangs of quarrelsome bummers."

FACTOID

On March 22, 1877, the National League published the first league-wide schedule in history.

The city of Chicago was so swept away by the success of the White Stockings that plans were set in motion to replace horse cars with steam cars on the transit route to the park in 1877—"an easy accommodation for businessmen to facilitate their being able to save time to do extra work on days they wished to go to the ball park," according to one newspaper article of the day.

All things considered, the first National League season was a fairly successful one, despite the domination of the White Stockings; the futility of the hapless Cincinnati Red Stockings, who managed just 5 wins as opposed to 56 losses; and the failure to complete the season's schedule by the Philadelphia Athletics and the New York Mutuals, who balked at making their final western trips, claiming they were economically strapped and could not afford to spend any more money.

William A. Hulbert replaced Morgan G. Bulkeley, who resigned as league president. At the December annual meeting of the National League, Hulbert demanded and received a unanimous vote to expel the wayward Mutuals and Athletics, even though they represented the league's two biggest cities. Both teams would not return to the league until Hulbert's death in 1882.

THE NATIONAL LEAGUE'S
SECOND SEASON AND FIRST SCANDAL

No replacements were named for the Mutuals and Athletics, and the National League moved into the 1877 season with six franchises. One outcome of the expulsion of the two teams was the creation of a uniform playing schedule. The entire league was required to adhere to it, a brilliant idea that made the game of baseball even more standardized and ceremonious. Now fans and newspaper reporters would know in advance the dates of all "home" and "away" games played by teams. The creation of two minor leagues—the International Association and the League Alliance—that 1877 season also saw the beginning of an organized baseball structure.

That 1877 season was also the summer of the first major scandal in baseball. After winning games early in the season, the Louisville Grays surprisingly lost seven games in a row. Players became out of sorts—clumsy, bobbling balls, swinging wide, loping slowly around the bases. Some were seen sporting expensive diamond stickpins. Newspaper editorials and stories were full of negative speculation about the team's sudden losses.

It was finally revealed that gamblers had paid off four team members, including Jim "Terror" Devlin, a top pitcher. It was said that each player collected $100 a game from the implicated gamblers. Confronted with the charge, Devlin confessed. He and the other players defending their actions blamed them on their owner who they claimed was not paying them money owed them.

The iron-fisted disciplinarian Hulbert, angered, ruthless, and prideful, took action. On October 30, 1877, he expelled the four Louisville players—James Devlin, George Hall, W. H. Craver, and

A. H. Nichols—from baseball for life for "crooked play" and "for conduct in the contravention of the objects of the league."

By 1881, Hulbert had received various pleas for reinstatement of the players. Unmoved, he dictated a note stating that for once and all the penalties inflicted on the players for their dishonest actions would never be remitted, nor would the league thereafter "entertain any appeal on the players' behalf."

Doggedly, Devlin attempted for five years to be reinstated, to no avail. Ironically, he took a job as a Philadelphia policeman. In 1883, he passed away from consumption. One newspaper claimed his death was "the fruits of crookedness."

The banning of players for life was just one facet of the toughness that pervaded National League policies. From its inception the league had a "blacklist"—a policy in force that enabled a team to release or discharge a player, no matter the reason. Other teams then went along with the unwritten code of refusing to negotiate for that released player's services. More and more, the blacklist became a weapon of the owners. At one stage in the early 1880s, 34 players and one umpire fell victim to it.

FACTOID

The Hop Bitters out of Rochester, New York, were one of the many barnstorming teams that came into vogue around 1880. The team was owned by the maker of a patent medicine known as Hop Bitters (advertised as the Invalid's Friend & Hope). Allegedly players prior to game were given a dose of the medicine—the reason, it was claimed, the team hardly ever lost a game.

COMPETITION FOR THE NATIONAL LEAGUE

The establishment National League hardly ever lost out to a challenge to break its monopoly in the 19th century. There were several pretenders to the throne, rival leagues. The American Base Ball Association was the most successful of the bunch. It lasted from 1882 to 1891.

Several factors accounted for the American Association's success. It charged only 25 cents a ticket—half the admission fee of the National League—and Sunday baseball was allowed, as well as the sale of liquor at games. It also inaugurated a percentage system to determine pennant winners. Back then it was an innovative and even controversial gesture; now, team standings based on won and lost percentages are commonplace in all sports.

The American Association also had the advantage of a wider population base than the older league. Charter franchises included Baltimore, Cincinnati, Louisville, Philadelphia, Pittsburgh, and St. Louis. Four of the six directors of those franchises owned breweries. The National League attacked the Association as a "Beer and Whiskey League" or the "Beer Ball League" because of the beer connection and because the new league attracted larger, more rowdy crowds, mainly immigrants and working-class men whose only had Sunday as a day off from work. The middle-class, native-born fans stayed loyal to the establishment National League.

It was actually the issue of beer that had triggered the creation of the American Association. In 1881, the National League objected to the Cincinnati team's selling beer in its ballpark. Worcester was the biggest complainer among the National League teams and insisted that the Reds discontinue their "distasteful practice."

The entire city of "Old Zinzinnati" was outraged at the antibeer stand, and a Cincy newspaper reflected the militant mood: "Puritanical Worcester is not liberal Cincinnati by a jugful and what is sauce for Worcester is wind for the Queen City. Beer and Sunday amusements have become a popular necessity in Cincinnati."

W. H. Kennett, president of the Cincinnati club, was adamant on the drinking issue and informed his colleagues in the National League that they could take Cincinnati with beer or not at all. It was not at all.

Miffed but anxious to get even, Cincinnati called together delegates from cities excluded from the National League and on November

2, 1881, formed the American Association of Base Ball Clubs. Charter members were Brooklyn, Cincinnati, Louisville, Pittsburgh, and St. Louis. Baltimore later replaced Brooklyn and Philadelphia joined the Association prior to the first season in 1882.

The new league went to war against the older circuit, extending invitations to National League players to become part of the American Association. Several players jumped leagues, prompting court battles and bitter diatribes between principals of both organizations. They really did not like each other, either.

Cincinnati won the first association pennant and began play against the Chicago White Sox, the National League pennant winner, in a postseason competition. The series, however, was stopped after two games had been played when the Association president threatened to expel the Reds for playing baseball with the "enemy."

In the midst of all the acrimony and hostility of the time, the man some referred to as the "Father of the National League" died. William Hulbert succumbed to heart problems on April 10, 1882. For his contributions, Hulbert was elected to the Hall of Fame by the Committee on Baseball Veterans in 1995. His plaque reads:

WILLIAM AMBROSE HULBERT
WAVY-HAIRED, SILVER-TONGUED EXECUTIVE AND
ENERGETIC, INFLUENTIAL LEADER. WHILE PART-
OWNER OF CHICAGO NATIONAL ASSOCIATION TEAM,
WAS INSTRUMENTAL IN FOUNDING NATIONAL LEAGUE
IN 1876. ELECTED N.L. PRESIDENT LATER THAT YEAR
AND IS CREDITED WITH ESTABLISHING RESPECTABILITY,
INTEGRITY AND SOUND FOUNDATION FOR NEW LEAGUE
WITH HIS RELENTLESS OPPOSITION TO BETTING, ROWDINESS,
AND OTHER PREVALENT ABUSES WHICH WERE
THREATENING THE SPORT

Two days later Albert Goodwill Spalding was among those who helped lower Hulbert's coffin into the ground. Moving on to purchase Hulbert's holdings in the club and becoming president of the Chicago team, the driven Spalding assumed principal ownership along with John Walsh, a prominent Chicago banker. Presiding now over the White Stockings, Spalding wielded power similar to that Hulbert once held over the National League.

FACTOID

In 1882 the American Association introduced color-coded uniforms hoping to help new fans learn the players' positions (the players called them "clown suits"). Second basemen wore orange and black.

Interleague warfare escalated early in 1883 when weak franchises in Troy and Worcester were dropped by the National League and replaced by New York and Philadelphia. The plan of the National League was for these franchises to go head-to-head against the Association teams in those cities. That 1883 season the National League regulated stockings for the first time. Teams were required to sport designated colors: Boston red, Buffalo gray, Chicago white, Cleveland blue, Providence light blue, Detroit brown, Philadelphia blue and white checks, and New York crimson and black.

Before the 1883 season began, a "harmony conference" was organized in New York City among representatives of the National League, the American Association, and the Northwestern League, a minor league that operated in Michigan, Ohio, and Illinois.

A. G. Mills, Hulbert's successor as National League president, represented the league. Elias Mather was the spokesman for the Northwestern League, and Denny McKnight presided for the American Association. A tripartite National Agreement was signed, honoring the contracts of each of the leagues. The agreement's main points were mutual recognition of reserved players and the setting up of exclusive territorial rights. Mills also announced that the National League recognized the American Association as having major league status. What would happen there would provide an interesting footnote to baseball history. The Northwestern League was to be endowed with the rank of a high minor league.

Still more organizational strife swirled around professional baseball late in 1883 when the Union Association came into being. The new league claimed that the reserve clause was a form of slavery and began to solicit players from the National League and the American Association. However, the new group's greatest success was in obtaining players from the weak Northwestern League. A blacklist was created by organized baseball to counter the Union Association. Under its provisions, in theory any player who jumped to the new league would be banned from baseball for life. The Union Association had a total of 34 teams. Eight cities had two competing Union Association teams; Philadelphia had three.

This unwieldy structure of too many teams in addition to the power of the existing leagues proved too much of a handicap for the Union Association. It collapsed after the 1884 season, with total losses of almost $250,000.

In 1885, the National League began its season with founding franchise members: Boston Beaneaters, Chicago White Stockings, Buffalo Bisons, Detroit Wolverines, New York Giants, Philadelphia Quakers, and Providence Grays.

After the Union Association folded, the Cleveland Spiders and St. Louis Unions merged into a new National League franchise, the latter renamed the St. Louis Maroons. Union Association President Henry V. Lucas, a young St. Louis millionaire, whose team played in the 10,000-seat "Palace Park of America," had romped to the 1884 pennant. Lucas was allowed to enter the National League with his St. Louis team, to the consternation of American Association leaders, especially St. Louis Browns owner Chris Von der Ahe, who now had a franchise vying directly with his for hometown support. However, Von der Ahe breathed easier when he was told that Lucas's Maroons would not be allowed to charge 25 cents for admission, play Sunday ball, or sell beer at the ballpark. Lucas's Union Association supporters felt betrayed, but they moved on to other projects, like forming the Western League early in 1885—the organization out of which the American League would come. At the conclusion of the season, the Bisons and Grays would drop out and be replaced by the Washington Senators and Kansas City Cowboys.

Both the American Association and National League set a maximum pay cap at $2,000 with no bonuses in 1885. That sparked the creation of the first major union of players—the Brotherhood of Professional Base Ball Players. The goals of that organization were to do away with the salary ceiling, modify the reserve clause, and make conditions more palatable for players. The preamble of the organization's constitution promised: "To protect and benefit ourselves collectively and individually. To promote a high standard of professional conduct. To foster and encourage the interests of . . . base ball."

The "reserve clause" was the most restrictive and controlling measure ever put into effect by the owners. In 1879 the owners had engaged in a secret pact to "reserve as property" their five best players. These athletes were not permitted to move to any other team. By 1883 11 players per team became reserved, and four years later the entire 14-man squad of each National League roster was reserved.

William A. Hulbert had argued the merits of the reserve clause thusly: the National League being "a business coalition . . . a perfectly just and proper stroke of business."

Players had no reason to view the reserve clause as just or even proper, but the system was a lifesaver for the owners. It gave them total power to terminate contracts and ban players from the previous practice of annual bargaining with other teams. With the reserve clause as a legal tool, owners were able to trade, sell, or drop a player. The athlete who balked at these conditions had just two alternatives: either try and tolerate them, or give up his baseball career.

Within a year of its creation, the Brotherhood boasted a membership of 107. John Montgomery Ward was the leader of the group. In 1879 Ward, as a pitcher for Providence, had posted a 44–18 record. He had pitched a perfect game on June 17, 1880. Later he became a switch-hitting star infielder for the New York Giants. A handsome, moneyed sophisticate, Ward was married to a beautiful actress. With all these things going for him, Ward could have easily walked away from bitter battles with owners and the vexing responsibilities of leadership of the Brotherhood, but he persisted out of a deep-felt sense of principle.

The owners dug in for the battle. They bribed newspaper editors to slant stories in their favor and to discredit the Brotherhood players, whom they called "hot-headed anarchists" and worse. Albert Spalding headed a "war committee" which threatened some athletes and bribed others to put down the player rebellion. Calumny, vulgarity—all were heaped on the Brotherhood, but Ward and his supporters persisted in their battle for reform, and in some states even won court cases against the reserve clause. However, these decisions were never able to be enforced.

When the 1888 season came to an end, National League club owners escalated their attempts at control. They adopted a classification plan—a kind of rating system for players based on their skills. The salary range was from $2,500 for Class A players down to $1,500 for Class E players. The action of the owners angered players, who at first threatened to strike. Then they backed away and appointed an arbitration committee, attempting to convince the owners to do away with the classification system. Confrontation led to threats, and threats led to hard-line positions on both sides.

All the fighting came to a head on November 4, 1889, when the Players National League of Baseball Clubs was formed to begin play in the 1890 season. The Players League had franchises slated for Boston, Brooklyn, Buffalo, Chicago, Cleveland, New York, Philadelphia, and Pittsburgh. Approximately 80 percent of the National League players went over to the new league, including the entire Washington team.

Adrian "Cap" Anson of the Chicago White Stockings and Philadelphia manager Harry Wright were two of the National League legends who refused to go to the new league. However, other big names did jump.

Albert G. Spalding was authorized by the National League to "go after big game." Spalding chose as his target Mike Kelly, "the King," then at the zenith of his career. The lively ballplayer was offered $10,000 and a three-year contract by Spalding. Spalding also gave Kelly a blank check and told him to fill in the amount himself.

"What does this mean?" Kelly asked Spalding, according to newspaper accounts at the time. "Does it mean that I'm to join the league? Quit the Brotherhood? Go back on the boys?"

"That's just what it means," responded Spalding. "It means that you go to Boston tonight."

"I must have time to think about this," said Kelly.

"There is mighty little time," Spalding pressed him. "If you don't want the money, somebody else will get it. When can you let me know?"

"In an hour and a half."

Kelly returned after spending the 90 minutes walking and thinking.

"Have you decided?" Spalding asked.

"Yes. I decided not to accept."

"What?" Spalding was taken by surprise. "You don't want the ten thousand dollars?"

"Aw, I want the ten thousand bad enough," said Kelly, "but I've thought the matter all over, and I can't go back on the boys. And neither would you. I'm with the Brotherhood."

Those "with the "Brotherhood" believed in its basic tenet: an idealistic attempt at cooperative capitalism. All players were given three-year contracts. A senate of 16 players, two representing each team, was organized. All teams placed $2,500 into a $20,000 prize fund, to be distributed to teams after the season, with the first-place team to receive $7,000. Another key element of the new league was the provision that if any team made a profit of more than $10,000, the additional profit would be divided equally among all the players in the league. It was a grand experiment in owner-and-player-shared profits and management. Unfortunately, like many grand experiments, it failed.

Although the brand of baseball played in the Players League was more skillful and more attractive than in the National League, although the new league drew more fans into its ballparks that 1890 season than the National League, although the established and wealthier National League lost almost twice as much money that disastrous 1890 season as the Players League, the established league had the resources to hold on and the Players League did not. Despite furious protests by members of the Brotherhood, key figures in the Players League worked out a settlement with the National League. The upstart league went under, and the National League simply bought up its players and investors. It was a classic case of a big fish eating a little fish.

"Baseball is a business," observed John Montgomery Ward, "not simply a sport." It was a statement that would echo across the decades to come.

"The baseball war of 1890," noted Connie Mack,

> threatened to throw both the National League and the Brotherhood League into bankruptcy. The magnates dropped about four million dollars in their desperate attempt to break the Brotherhood; finally, at great cost, they succeeded. Players scrambled back to their old magnates. They had been suspended for life, but "life" was a relative term in that time and context. They were received with open arms when they came back as prodigal sons. . . . But the Brotherhood had started a new era in baseball. Club owners had awakened to the realization that ballplayers are human and must be given a fair deal or they will rebel.

INTERLEAGUE CHAMPIONSHIPS

Booming prosperity in the 1880s enabled baseball to boom at the turnstiles in both the National League and the American Association. The forerunner of the World Series—postseason competition between the two leagues—was in place. However, it was a fumbling, bumbling kind of competition that represented the scatter-gun organization and divisiveness of 19th-century baseball.

In 1884, the Providence Grays, National League pennant winner—decided on a percentage basis for the first time—and the New York Metropolitans of the American Association staged a best-of-five-game postseason series. Behind phenomenal pitcher Charles "Old Hoss" Radbourn, who pitched the first three games and won all of them, the Grays won the "world championship." Providence now had bragging rights that it had put the upstart American Association in its place.

That series created a precedent for postseason play between National League and American Association pennant winners over the next half-dozen seasons. In 1885 the National League Chicago White Stockings and the St. Louis Browns of the American Association met in postseason competition—with $1,000 dollars in prize money slated for the winner. The competition was a cross between a World Series and a barnstorming tour, as games were played in Chicago, St. Louis, Pittsburgh, and Cincinnati. There was violence in the stands and on the field, disputes with umpires, slanted news coverage in the press. And when all the fighting, fussing, and playing were over, the final results were murky. Some argued that each team had won three games. Others felt that the Browns were the champs three games to two, since the first game was ruled a forfeit. Chicago recognized the forfeit, but the Browns ignored it. The bottom line was that both owners were content to stop the mad on-field activity after six games rather than go on to a decisive seventh contest. The prize money was equally divided between the two teams and so was the anger players on both clubs felt for each other.

Chicago's Cap Anson claimed that he doubted the Browns could finish even as high as fifth place in the National League. An incensed Bobby Caruthers, St. Louis pitcher, waved a roll of bills at Anson. "I'll bet you one thousand dollars," he shouted, "that the Browns can easily beat your nine. And I'll put this money up as a forfeit."

Chicago shortstop Ned Williamson intervened: "We White Stockings," he snapped, "stand ready to cover all bets the Brown Stockings wish to make."

When the 1886 season came to a close, it was clear that the White Stockings were the class of the National League and the

Browns once again were the premier club in the American Association. Chicago finished the season with a 90–34 record, winning 24 of its last 34 games; the Browns posted a 93–46 record, winding up their regular season a dozen games in front of second-place Pittsburgh.

The star of St. Louis was Bobby Caruthers, just 5' 7" and 138 pounds, dubbed "Mighty Mite." Winner of 30 of his 44 pitching decisions, he also found time to play the outfield and bat .342. Caruthers had a 218–99 record through nine seasons to 1892.

Charles Comiskey was the playing manager of the Browns. Master of the taunt and the tease, he took up a position as close to home plate as possible and unleashed lengthy diatribes and short shots of vulgarity at the opposition, especially catchers.

The larger-than-life hero of the White Stockings was Michael "King" Kelly, who batted a National League–leading .388 in 1886 and, according to newspaper reports, "could get the nomination for mayor of Chicago on any ticket without making any effort."

The championship series, advertised as "the world's championship," between the two veteran teams called for seven games in seven days—three in Chicago, three in St. Louis, and the seventh game, if necessary, at a neutral site: Cincinnati. The compactly scheduled competition was necessary due to previous commitments by the Browns, who had arranged to play a best-of-nine series commencing October 14 against their National League counterparts, the St. Louis Maroons.

The Browns went to work on their rigorous postseason schedule, winning four straight from the Maroons, then interrupting that series to begin their series against the White Stockings. Yes, that was baseball back then!

The first four games between the Browns and White Stockings were split; lots of high scoring took place, as well as an experiment in umpiring. The first and third games were officiated by one arbiter. The second and fourth games saw each club appoint an umpire of its choice. These umps were backed up by a referee, "Honest John" Kelly, who was on the scene to straighten out any disagreements between the umpires.

The fourth game was a controversial affair. Second baseman Fred Pfeffer of Chicago allowed a one-out, bases-loaded pop-up to drop in the sixth inning (this was a normal attempt to initiate a double play in those days before the creation of the infield fly rule). However, Pfeffer not only failed to start a double play, he manhandled the baseball, opening things up for the underdog Browns to come away with an 8–5 triumph.

Fans and bettors were furious, claiming that the championship series was a hippodrome, a fix, that the White Stockings were allowing the series to extend to make for larger gate receipts in the winner-take-all competition. Cap Anson was furious at the charges. "These games are for blood," he shot back at the allegations of hippo-droming. "These games are for the world championship."

The fifth game of the series saw the Browns rout the White Stockings, 10–3, in a game that was stopped after seven innings because of darkness. Al Spalding had to use shortstop Ned Williamson as a starting pitcher and outfielder Jimmy Ryan as a relief pitcher in that contest because of a suddenly sore-armed and exhausted pitching staff.

An excited crowd of 10,000 showed up at Sportsman's Park in St. Louis for the sixth game. The Browns wore white baseball suits with brown trim of imported English cricket flannel. The White Stockings came to the St. Louis park in horse-drawn carriages, the players decked out in royal blue uniforms, white caps, and long white socks. Underscoring the comment made by Anson, "It was clear to see," the *Sporting News* reported, "that [both teams] had come out for blood."

After seven innings, the White Stockings led 3–0. One of the runs scored on a fourth-inning long fly ball off the bat of Pfeffer into the right field seats. The ball was still considered in play by the rules of the competition, but the frantic Browns outfielder was not able to retrieve it in time to retire Pfeffer.

In the eighth inning, the Browns scored three runs to tie the score. Two runs came in on Arlie Latham's triple. The player, whose nickname was "The Freshest Man in the World," had yelled to the crowd as he came to bat: "Don't get nervous, folks, I'll tie it up."

In the St. Louis 10th, outfielder Curt Welch leaned his shoulder into a pitch to get hit by the ball and started to first base. Chicago catcher King Kelly protested. Welch was forced to bat over. He singled, and with one out was on third base. White Stocking pitching ace John Clarkson watched as Welch danced up and down the baseline. Then Clarkson quick-pitched the batter and the ball sailed over catcher Kelly's head. Welch slid home with the winning run. The Browns had defeated the White Stockings, and Welch's run became known, hyperbolically, as the "$15,000 slide."

The next day the Browns defeated the Maroons in the climactic but also anticlimactic game of their local championship competition. King Kelly made a presentation to the Browns in the fifth inning of that game against the Maroons. "They have earned it," said a reportedly sober Kelly. "They have beaten our club fairly. We hope to meet them again in the future."

Chris Von der Ahe, the St. Louis owner, wanted to play the scheduled seventh game of the World Championship as an exhibition game in Cincinnati. However, Albert Spalding would have no more of the Browns. "We know when we've had enough," he telegraphed Von der Ahe. The teams operated under a winner-take-all formula which awarded the Browns $13,000 for the series. The paunchy Von der Ahe graciously gave each of his players $580 and pocketed the rest. The St. Louis owner had the satisfaction of his team's having defeated the heavily favored Chicago White Stockings of the National League as well as the pride of driving around his city for months in a carriage with horses draped with blankets adorned with the inscription "ST. LOUIS BROWNS, CHAMPIONS OF THE WORLD."

In 1887, Detroit challenged St. Louis of the American Association to a 15-game series staged in 10 different cities. Total attendance for the 15 games was only 51,455 and total gate dollars were even less. Fans and players were just worn out from all the rigors of a 15-game series. For the record, the Detroit National League team won 10 of the 15 games they played against the Browns.

The postseason competition was mercifully reduced to 10 games in 1888. The St. Louis Browns took the field against the New York

Nationals. St. Louis owner Chris Von der Ahe did it up big. He hired a special train for his players and guests. Viewing the baseball doings as one lavish party, the St. Louis beer baron bought a suit of clothes for each of his athletes and special guests. Celebrating with huge grogs of beer and other spirits made the St. Louis players feel no pain, but it did little for their athletic ability, and many wondered how St. Louis was able to win even four of the 10 games played. The total affair cost Von der Ahe almost $50,000, but he was philosophical about it all, claiming the entire thing "was lots of fun and a good investment."

Brooklyn of the American Association and the New York Nationals went head to head in more sedate postseason play in 1889, as the New Yorkers won, six games to three. In 1890, Louisville players claimed they were "tuckered out" and quit postseason play against the Brooklyn Nationals when their series was tied up at three all.

Although inconsistency of play, apathy, and lunacy of logistics reduced attendance in those 19th-century postseason encounters, they did plant the seeds for the World Series of the future. It was also the first time in the history of baseball that most teams operated in the black. Player salaries escalated accordingly as the two leagues waged an all-out battle for talent.

BASEBALL IN THE 1890S

Although the National Agreement was in place, it was often ignored. In the American Association, Brooklyn and St. Louis were perennial battlers for the pennant and control of the league's management. In 1890, a puppet of the St. Louis Browns was made president of the American Association. Brooklyn and Cincinnati then abandoned the Association and jumped to the National League, which ignored the principles of the National Agreement and readied itself for all-out battle against the American Association. That was also the year that the Players League came into being. Competing against two leagues was too much for the Association. In 1890 the Players League drew 980,888 and the National League attendance was 813,678, while the

Association was third with a reported 500,000. Its attendance in decline and some of its players departing for better pay, the Association was reeling. And on December 17, 1891, it was through—a footnote to baseball history.

Four of its clubs (St. Louis, Louisville, Washington, and Baltimore) were absorbed into what became a 12-team National League (as the "National League and American Association of Professional Base Ball Clubs"). The other four American Association clubs were bought out for about $130,000. The National League announced that it would allow Sunday games for the first time but would retain its 50-cent minimum admission price.

On the playing field, there were several historic moments. In 1894, Hugh Duffy of Boston batted an astounding .438. His teammate Bobby Lowe became the first man in history to hit four home runs in one game. A year later Ed Delahanty became the second player to hit four home runs in a game. "Big Ed" was presented with four boxes of chewing gum for his classic clouts.

That same season Delahanty (.407), Sam Thompson (.407), and Billy Hamilton (.404) all reached the .400 mark as outfielders for the Phillies. Combined, the trio batted .407 and averaged 199 hits, 149 runs, 120 RBI, 20 triples, 75 walks, and 48 stolen bases.

FACTOID

Ed Delahanty is the only player to have four brothers precede him in the major leagues—Jim Delahanty, Frank Delahanty, Joe Delahanty, and Tom Delahanty.

In 1897, "Wee Willie" Keeler hit safely in 44 straight games—a record that would endure for 44 seasons. And that 1897 season, a powerfully formed, bowlegged player made his National League debut. His name was Honus Wagner.

As the century drew toward its close, a myriad of problems, a quest for order, and a struggle for survival characterized the tone and the tempo of baseball. Only Chicago and Boston of the original National League franchises still fielded teams in 1890. Between 1877 and 1890, 23 different cities had been represented in the National League—a circuit which in that time period never had more than eight teams in one season.

As the final decade wore on, the National League continued to cope with huge debts that it had accumulated in its war with the Brotherhood. Additionally, the absorption of the four teams from the American Association created many burdens in the league's image and attendance. Louisville and St. Louis were the weak sisters of the National League; they drew very poorly. And the Giants of New York, a flagship franchise, were no longer competitive on the field, further weakening the strength of the National League.

Riotous behavior by players, a conspicuous use of indecent and obscene language, umpire baiting—all of these further tarnished the image of an unwieldy and obtuse 12-team National League throughout the 1890s. As the 19th century came to a close, political bickering among owners, a salary ceiling of $2,400 that infuriated players, lively competition from other entertainment sources, and the inability to consummate plans to create two six-team divisions all were part of the thick web of problems afflicting the National League scene.

And so was the franchise from Cleveland, a team that painfully revealed the league's imbalance. The players wore white and dark blue uniforms, and a club executive assessing their not-too-robust shape remarked: "They look skinny and spindly, just like spiders. Might as well call them Spiders and be done with it."

That pathetic aggregation won 20 games and lost 134 that 1899 season, for a winning percentage of .130, and finished dead, dead last—84 games behind pennant-winning Brooklyn. Cleveland's sorry pitching staff had a 30-game loser, a 22-game loser, and two hurlers who suffered 35 defeats between them. The Spiders were last in runs scored, doubles, triples, home runs, batting average, slugging percentage, and stolen bases. Only once that 1899 season did they win two games in a row, while on six occasions they had losing streaks of 11 or more games.

That year of 1899 was the final season of the Cleveland Spiders. The following winter the National League went back to eight teams; Cleveland, Washington, Louisville, and Baltimore were cut out.

BLACK PLAYERS IN THE NATIONAL LEAGUE AND CREATION OF THE NATIONAL COLORED LEAGUE

The National League granted major league status to the American Association for the 1884 season, a move that is a poignant postscript to 19th-century baseball enabling purists to maintain that the first blacks in major league baseball were the Walker brothers of Toledo, not Jackie Robinson, who broke the color line in the national pastime in 1947.

In 1883, Moses "Fleetwood" Walker, a catcher, signed with the Toledo Blue Stockings of the Northwestern League. A year later the Blue Stockings joined the American Association, now considered a major league. A former Oberlin College star, Fleetwood was a better-than-average hitter and among baseball's better catchers almost from the beginning of his career. But he and his brother were exposed to a horrific environment at Toledo. Walker's own teammates expressed annoyance and sometimes much more at having to play with him. Toledo's ace pitcher, Tony Mullane, admitted that Walker "was the best catcher I ever worked with, but I disliked a Negro and whenever I had to pitch to him I used to pitch anything I wanted without looking at his signals." Profane letters called for Walker's removal from the team. Even worse, their manager, C. H. Morton, received letters that threatened the life of the brothers. In Louisville, Fleetwood was forced to sit in the stands while his team played.

The most outspoken racist of the time was the multitalented Cap Anson, player-manager of Chicago. On July 20, 1884, his White Stockings agreed to play against the Mud Hens only after Toledo gave in to demands that Fleetwood Walker be kept off the field.

FACTOID

Richmond Virginia
September 5, 1884
Manager, Toledo Baseball Club

Dear Sir: We the undersigned, do hereby warn you not to put up [Moses "Fleet"] Walker, the Negro catcher, the days you play in Richmond, as we could mention the names of seventy-five determined men who have sworn to mob Walker, if he comes on the grounds in a suit [baseball uniform]. We hope you will listen to our words of warning, so there will be no trouble, and if you do not, there certainly will be. We only write this to prevent much bloodshed, as you alone can prevent.

[signed] Bill Frick, James Kendrick, Dynx Dunn, Bob Roseman

That 1884 season Walker's brother Welday managed to play in five games. Fleetwood Walker played in 46 games and batted .263, a fairly decent average for a catcher. It was claimed that his fielding was subpar and that he had a hand injury. Both claims were debatable, but he was let go. During that 1884 season the International League passed a resolution opposing its teams' participating in games against squads with black players. The pointed edict was directed at Buffalo, which had a black second baseman, Frank Grant, and Newark, which had a black pitcher, George Stovey.

Grant was one of the greatest African-American players of the 19th century. He had played on an all-white team in Meriden, Connecticut, in the Eastern League in the 1880s, never hitting below .313 in six seasons there. At age 20, he led the International League in hitting.

Stovey is deemed the first great black pitcher. In 1886 he was the top pitcher for Jersey City of the International League, holding opposing hitters to a .167 batting average. He moved to Newark in 1887 and went 34–14, setting a still-standing International League record for wins. He also played the outfield and hit .255.

In 1887, Fleetwood Walker along with Bud Fowler, Frank Grant, Robert Higgins, George Stovey, and three other black players joined Newark, New Jersey, in the newly organized International League. Racism was rampant. Black players were heckled and threatened by fans, ridiculed and ignored by teammates, vilified in the press.

The end of black players in organized baseball was clear. Most of the members of the St. Louis Browns refused to play a game against an all-black team that summer. An International League umpire announced that he would always rule against a team that included blacks. By 1890, there were no black players in the International League, the most prestigious of the minor league circuits. Finally, major league owners had a "gentleman's agreement" in place not to sign any more black players. Clubs stopped recruiting black players and soon they disappeared altogether from organized white baseball. Though black players found employment in lesser leagues, by the turn of the century the color barrier was firmly in place.

The antiblack feeling in baseball clearly revealed the prejudice of that era in the United States. Racists were fond of trotting out the phrase "chocolate-colored coons" to describe black baseball players. Players suspected of being black were taunted and run out of organized baseball. In the 1880s Lou Nava was forced out, and in the 1890s George Treadway received the same cruel treatment. There was never proof that either man was black—only a suspicion based on their appearance.

Harassed, discriminated against, African-American players continued to play ball on more than 200 all-black independent teams that existed all over the United States from the early 1880s forward. In 1885, the first all-black professional team was organized. They were called the "Cuban Giants"—even through the team was composed of African-Americans, not Cubans. Since the United States had friendly relations with Cuba then, it was thought the name would garner acceptance by white patrons. Frank P. Thompson, a headwaiter at the Argyle Hotel in Babylon, New York, was the impetus behind the team, pinnacle of black baseball in their time. They barnstormed against both white and black teams. To counter white prejudice, they reportedly communicated on the field in a kind of gibberish to fool the crowd into thinking they were speaking Spanish.

> "The Cuban Giants, the famous baseball club, have defeated the New Yorks, 4 games out of five, and are now virtually champions of the world. The St. Louis Browns, Detroits and Chicagos, afflicted with Negrophobia and unable to bear the odium of being beaten by colored men, refused to accept their challenge."
>
> —*Indianapolis Freeman*, 1888

Due to the success of the original Cuban Giants, many similar teams sprang up: the Genuine Cuban Giants, Royal Giants, the Baltimore Giants, Havana Giants, Harrisburg Giants, Philadelphia Orions, the Boston Resolutes, the Lord Baltimores of Baltimore, the St. Louis Black Stockings, the Gothams and Cuban X Giants from New York, and the Page Fence Giants from Adrian, Michigan, winners of 82 straight games in 1897.

In 1887, the National Colored League was created, with teams based in Louisville, New York, Philadelphia, Baltimore, Boston, and Cincinnati. In 1888, the Cuban Giants manhandled a top white team based in New York, winning four out of five games in the series. After that, white teams in Detroit, Chicago, and St. Louis refused to accept challenges to play against the Cuban Giants, not wishing to risk defeat at the hands of black men. That was little balm for the Cuban Giants and other black teams back then who were made to suffer all types of indignities, including being barred from many hotels and having to resort to sleeping on park benches.

> FACTOID
>
> Catcher Moses "Fleetwood" Walker and the man considered to have been the first great black pitcher, George Stovey, formed the first black battery in organized baseball with Newark (International League) in 1887.

THE NEW CENTURY AND THE ARRIVAL OF THE AMERICAN LEAGUE

As one century was ending and a new one was being born, baseball had evolved into a blend of hitting and pitching, defense and offense. It had changed radically from the way it was in its early years as a result of all the tinkering, refinements, and rules changes. Nuance and geometry were mixed and matched, and mixed and matched some more, making baseball more appealing to fans, more balanced for the players, more a game that would stake its claim as America's premier sport of the 20th century, the national pastime.

As the 20th century began, the pitcher threw overhand from the mound to the batter, who swung at a ball not nearly as lively as the one used today. Batters worked on the art and science of hitting, while base runners worked on their maneuvers on the bases. Catchers were stationed immediately behind home plate with regalia including mask, chest protector, and heavy mitt. The days of the gloveless wonders were all but gone; most fielders sported mitts of some type, skimpy and frail as they were compared to those in use today.

The National League had survived the challenge of other leagues like the American Base Ball Association and the Union Association. By the end of the 19th century, the National League controlled professional baseball in the United States.

Newspapers of the time covered the daily doings of baseball teams and their stars, who were rapidly becoming America's folk heroes. Journalistic baseball jargon, press partiality to the home team, and obsession by reporters with statistics were all part of the scene.

In the America of 1900, 31 million people lived in cities and 46 million dwelled in rural areas. In the America of 1900, the *New York Times* noted, "Rowdyism by the players on the field, syndicalism among the club owners, poor umpiring and talk of rival organizations . . . are the principal causes for baseball's decline."

In 1900 the reorganized eight-team National League consisted of Boston, Brooklyn, Chicago, Cincinnati, New York, Philadelphia, Pittsburgh, and St. Louis. It was a pattern that would remain intact until 1953—those eight teams of the National League whose names virtually every schoolboy would be able to recite by heart.

It was back in 1893 when Byron Bancroft Johnson, known as Ban, then president of the Western League—the strongest and most solvent of the minor leagues—began to dream his dream of a second major league. With his league's franchises located in the Midwest and his lieutenant Charles Comiskey heading the successful St. Paul club, the former sportswriter Johnson believed that he could succeed where others had failed in achieving parity with the National League. The Western League differed sharply in ambience from the old second major league: no liquor was allowed in the ballparks, player decorum was monitored, umpires were supported, and attendance by women was encouraged.

In 1900, Ban Johnson renamed his league the American League and asked the National League to classify his new circuit as a major league. His request was met with scorn and ridicule by the National League moguls; they had been through this sort of thing before.

Johnson explained that his desire for major league status for the American League was motivated by "self-preservation." He also explained that his new league would provide protection for the National League against the actions of other groups who might be unfriendly to the Nationals. Finally, Johnson maintained that "we in the American [League] wish to act wholly in concert with the National and on absolutely friendly terms."

The National League showed its disdain for the new American League and its request for major league status by having its secretary, Nick Young, send a letter to Johnson asking the new league to remit its fees—a traditional bit of homage for minor leagues. Johnson sent a letter but no fees back to Young. In his letter Johnson explained that no fees were being paid to the National League because the American League considered itself a viable major league candidate. "We will become a major league, whether the Nationals wish it or not," said Johnson. He also made it clear that his new league planned to expand into eastern (National) territory in 1901.

When the 1900 season ended, Johnson appointed a "circuit committee" made up of himself, Charles Comiskey, now the Chicago team owner, and Charles Somers, owner of the Cleveland club. The mission of the committee was to survey selected cities in the East "as to their appropriate baseball backgrounds."

Connie Mack secured backing for an American League franchise in Philadelphia. The owner of the 1900 Milwaukee team agreed to support its transfer to Washington. And Wilbert Robinson and John McGraw announced that they would sponsor a team in Baltimore.

A Boston group also was eager to finance a team for 1901. But Boston was virtually sacred National League territory, and rather than push too hard, Johnson told National League leaders that he wished to meet with them to discuss all possibilities. The December 1900 National League conference was designated as the place for the meeting. Johnson was kept waiting for hours outside the door of the National League conference. Finally, the Nationals, completing their business, slipped out a side door, ignoring Johnson.

An announcement was made to the press that the National League would operate a new minor league in the Midwest in 1901 and would include Minneapolis and Kansas City as part of the operation. The National League announcement was a dagger pointed directly at the American League. White with anger, Johnson snarled. "Well, if they want a real war, they can have war."

In 1901 Johnson claimed official major league status for his new league and yet another baseball war was on. The 1901 American League teams were Chicago, Detroit, Milwaukee, and Cleveland in the West; Boston, Baltimore, Washington, and Philadelphia in the East. The lure of money—more money than the $2,400 National League salary ceiling—brought some of the brightest stars into the

American League: Cy Young, Joe McGinnity, Napoleon Lajoie, John McGraw, Jimmie Collins, Wee Willie Keeler, Bobby Wallace, Ed Delahanty, Jack Chesbro . . .

The new American League honored contracts but chose to ignore the reserve clause. At least 70 players ultimately moved over to the American League, which drew more than 2,000,000 fans in 1902, to fewer than 1,700,000 for the National League. Finally, after two years of financial losses, the National League owners reluctantly agreed to sue for peace with the American League. The Nationals sought to consolidate both leagues into a 12-team circuit, but Johnson refused. In the final peace settlement—the National Agreement of 1902—the American League was permitted to retain most of the players who had come over from the National League. The two circuits then agreed to honor each other's reserve rights and contracts. The new agreement also protected the minor leagues: their territorial rights were secured, and they were granted reserve rights for players. And a system was enacted that set up machinery for major league teams to draft players from minor league teams and pay the minor league teams for the contracts of these players.

In essence, peace between the National League and the American League solidified baseball's business foundation, consolidated all the gains of the sport in the 19th century, and set the tone for all the baseball that would follow.

In baseball's first action shot, Union troops stand in parade formation at Fort Pulaski, Savannah, Georgia, 1862 or 1863, before a baseball game in progress. (Courtesy of the National Baseball Hall of Fame Library, Cooperstown, NY)

Two men fundamental to baseball's beginnings: Alexander Cartwright, Jr. *(left)*, the actual father of the game (here shown, circa 1870, as the fire chief of Honolulu, where he later settled); and Albert Spalding *(below)*, circa 1875, pitcher par excellence and later baseball's premier entrepreneur. (Courtesy of the National Baseball Hall of Fame Library, Cooperstown, NY)

John Montgomery Ward, one of baseball's first superstars: pitcher, infielder, outfielder, switch-hitter, lawyer, and a founder of baseball's first players' union, the Brotherhood of Professional Base Ball Players, in 1879. (Courtesy of the National Baseball Hall of Fame Library, Cooperstown, NY)

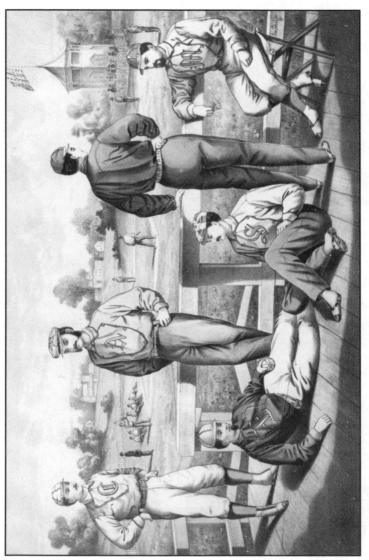

Baseball fashions: what the teams of the 1870s wore. The first team to adopt shortened pants was the Cincinnati Red Stockings. (Courtesy of the National Baseball Hall of Fame Library, Cooperstown, NY)

Moses Fleetwood Walker *(above)*, baseball's
first black major-league player, in 1884.
Both Fleetwood and his brother Welday
were educated at Oberlin College, Ohio
(they are pictured below in Oberlin's first
varsity baseball team: Fleetwood, number 6,
Welday, number 10). Both played for the
Toledo Mudhens until Adrian "Cap" Anson
(right), the legendary player-manager of the
Chicago White Stockings in the 1880s and
the most powerful racist in the business,
demanded that Fleetwood be removed
from the field. (Courtesy of the National
Baseball Hall of Fame Library,
Cooperstown, NY)

The Providence Grays, 1884 National League champions and winner of the first postseason competition, winning the best of five games over the New York Metropolitans. (Courtesy of the National Baseball Hall of Fame Library, Cooperstown, NY)

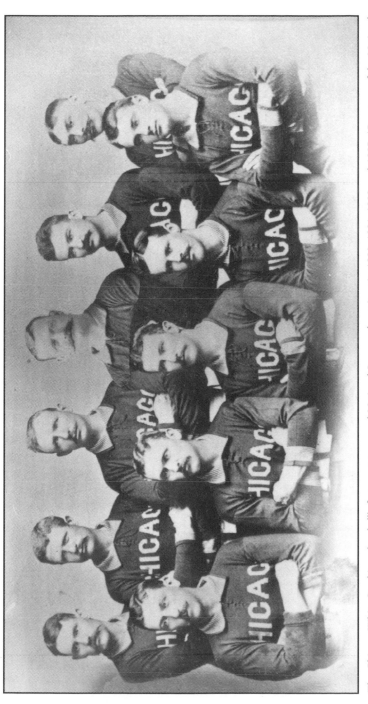

The Chicago White Stockings, baseball's first great team and National League champions in 1880, 1881, 1882, and 1885. (Courtesy of the National Baseball Hall of Fame Library, Cooperstown, NY)

The St. Louis Browns, who won four straight American Association pennants, 1885–1888, and were champions of the world in 1886. Pictured in group photo in 1888, with the inspirational player-manager Charles Comiskey in the center. (Courtesy of the National Baseball Hall of Fame Library, Cooperstown, NY)

The New York Giants, National League champions of 1889. (Courtesy of the National Baseball Hall of Fame Library, Cooperstown, NY)

Players at the Sphinx, during Al Spalding's baseball missionary effort to the world in 1889. The tour went to Hawaii, Australia, New Zealand, Egypt, Italy, France, and Britain, playing exhibition games. Spalding took it upon himself to educate both royalty and the crowds in the rules of the game—doing a bit of marketing along the side for his Spalding bats, balls, gloves, and uniforms. (Courtesy of the National Baseball Hall of Fame Library, Cooperstown, NY)

The Young Ladies Baseball Club No. 1, 1890–1891. The team traveled from city to city, playing exhibition games against themselves or against men's teams. While there is some question whether all the young ladies were indeed female, the games nonetheless attracted crowds as well as press censure—baseball was not a seemly sport for Victorian young ladies. (Courtesy of the National Baseball Hall of Fame Library, Cooperstown, NY)

John McGraw, a major force behind three Baltimore pennants in the 1890s, in warm-up gear. (Courtesy of the National Baseball Hall of Fame Library, Cooperstown, NY)

The Boston South End Grounds, which burned down on May 15, 1894. Spectators had been distracted by a fight involving McGraw at third base, then fled to the field for safety as the fire raged. Miraculously no one was hurt, though the fire claimed some 150 homes in the vicinity. (Courtesy of the National Baseball Hall of Fame Library, Cooperstown, NY)

From the Baltimore Orioles' great 1890s team, a team heavy with Irish players: *standing,* Joe Kelley, John McGraw, and an unidentified player; *seated,* Hughie Jennings and Wee Willie Keeler. (Courtesy of the National Baseball Hall of Fame Library, Cooperstown, NY)

The Baltimore Orioles, pennant winners in 1894, 1895, and 1896, surrounding manager Ned Hanlon. (Courtesy of the National Baseball Hall of Fame Library, Cooperstown, NY)

Albert Spalding, the senior statesman and entrepreneur of baseball, circa 1900. (Courtesy of the National Baseball Hall of Fame Library, Cooperstown, NY)

FIVE

Tintypes: A Sampler

Baseball is a man maker.
—Al Spalding

They peer out of faded photographs, some have mustaches and others have beards and still others have the clean-shaven faces of innocents playing ball in a less sophisticated time. They were the pioneers of a sport, the trailblazers.

CAP ANSON

There were many remarkable aspects to the career of Adrian Constantine (the given names were for his father's favorite towns in Michigan) "Cap" Anson. But his racism, avowed and blatant, cannot be ignored. Once, he pulled his ball club off the field protesting playing a team that had a black player. And it was said that he kept his influence and prejudice going against black players throughout his 27-year playing career.

But if race relations was his low point, baseball was a lofty aspect of his life. He was the first great star in National League history, a towering figure who batted .313 lifetime. The slugging first baseman–manager of the Chicago White Stockings batted better than .300 19 times in his 22-year major league career. Anson also was the first player in major league history to record 3,000 hits—ending his career with exactly 3,000.

At age 19, the Iowan turned pro in 1871 with the Rockford Forest Citys of the National Association (NA), the forerunner of the National League (NL). The following season, he joined the Philadelphia Athletics as a third baseman and first baseman. In five NA seasons, he hit over .350 four times. One of the first players signed by William Hulbert when he launched the National League in 1876, Anson helped the Chicago team (then called White Stockings) to the first NL pennant, hitting .356. He once hit five home runs in two days in an era when even slamming one homer was a rarity. He also was the first player to hit three consecutive home runs in one game, the first to notch four straight doubles in game, the first first baseman to record two unassisted double plays in a single game.

"Round up the strongest men who can knock a baseball the farthest the most often, put yourself on first base and win."

—Cap Anson

In 1879, Anson became a player-manager. Chicago fans adored him; his players did not. He imposed bed checks, levied fines for beer drinking, and hired Pinkerton detectives to follow players he suspected of backsliding. Anson's loud, annoying, bellowing voice intimidated players and umpires alike.

On sheer talent, Hall of Fame induction came to him in 1939. His plaque reads:

Adrian Constantine Anson
"CAP"
GREATEST HITTER AND GREATEST
NATIONAL LEAGUE PLAYER-MANAGER
OF 19TH CENTURY. STARTED WITH
CHICAGOS IN NATIONAL LEAGUE'S
FIRST YEAR 1876. CHICAGO MANAGER
FROM 1879 TO 1897 WINNING 5 PENNANTS.
BATTING CHAMPION 4 TIMES.

His desire was that his epitaph should read: "Here lies a man who batted .300." Innovator, iconoclast, inspired leader of the Colts of Chicago, Adrian Constantine Anson was much more than just a man who batted .300.

DAN BROUTHERS

The premier power hitter of his era, Dan Brouthers led his league six times in batting, seven times in slugging average, four times in total bases, three times in doubles, twice in homers, and once in triples. His .519 lifetime slugging average surpassed that of the next-best 19th-century slugger by a substantial margin. He played on five pennant winners with five different teams in four different leagues— Troy Trojans (1879–1880), Buffalo Bisons (1881–1885), Detroit Wolverines (1886–1888), Boston Beaneaters (1889), Boston Reds (1890–1891), Brooklyn Grooms (1892–1893), Baltimore Orioles (1894–1895), Louisville Colonels (1895), Philadelphia Phillies (1896), New York Giants (1904)

The man who was the "Babe Ruth of his day" at 6 feet, 2 inches and 207 pounds, Brouthers personified power hitting. His 1886 clout out of Washington's Capitol Park was the storied tape measure shot of its era. That same year Brouthers smashed a home run out of the ballpark in Boston that banged into Sullivan's Tower, scattering fans who up to that point thought they had a safe, free, and unobstructed view of the game.

The first player to win back-to-back batting titles (1882 and 1883), Brouthers had a chance at three in a row in 1884, but a sprained ankle got in the way. The powerfully built first baseman batted .300 or more 14 times and compiled a lifetime batting average of .343. At the advanced baseball age of 48, Dennis "Dan" Brouthers was still plying his trade in the high minor leagues.

In 1945 the Veterans Committee of the Hall of Fame selected several "old-timers" to recognize the early days of baseball. Brouthers was among that group. His plaque reads:

DAN BROUTHERS

HARD-HITTING FIRST BASEMAN OF

EIGHT MAJOR LEAGUE CLUBS, HE WAS

PART OF ORIGINAL "BIG FOUR" OF BUFFALO.

TRADED WITH OTHER MEMBERS OF

THAT COMBINATION TO DETROIT, HE HIT

.419 AS CITY WON ITS ONLY NATIONAL

LEAGUE CHAMPIONSHIP IN 1887.

JESSE BURKETT

Jesse Burkett was born on December 4, 1868, in Wheeling, West Virginia, and grew up to be only 5 feet, 8 inches tall, if one measured generously, and 155 pounds and all short fuse. He was known as "the Crab," a nickname his not-too-genial personality earned for him. Some observers noted that Burkett, an insulter of opposing players, an inciter of fans, was a one-man riot. "Other players are bigger and huskier," the outspoken Burkett explained. "I have to make up for the difference somehow."

He played for the New York Giants (1890), Cleveland Spiders (1891–1898), St. Louis Perfectos/Cardinals (1899–1901), St. Louis Browns (1902–1904), and Boston Red Sox (1905)—making his career one that spanned baseball in two different centuries. He shares the distinction along with Rogers Hornsby and Ty Cobb of being the only player in baseball history to bat .400 or better three times. A batting champion in 1895 (.423) and 1896 (.410), Burkett also batted .402 in 1899, but lost his chance for another batting crown that season because Philadelphia's Ed Delahanty batted .408. Burkett was one of baseball's most exceptional bunters and batted leadoff through most of his career.

A left-handed line-drive hitter with a practiced ability to foul pitches off, Burkett's skill was one of the reasons for the introduction of the rule making foul balls strikes. He said he owed his success to "that old confeedence," but his speed helped him leg out many hits. He scored more than 100 runs in nine different seasons.

Burkett was elected to the Hall of Fame by the Committee on Baseball Veterans in 1946. His plaque reads:

> JESSE C. BURKETT
> BATTING STAR WHO PLAYED OUTFIELD FOR
> THE NEW YORK, CLEVELAND AND ST. LOUIS
> N.L. TEAMS AND THE ST. LOUIS AND BOSTON
> A.L. TEAMS. SHARES WITH ROGERS HORNSBY
> AND TY COBB THE RECORD OF HITTING .400
> OR BETTER THE MOST TIMES. ACCOMPLISHED
> THIS ON THREE OCCASIONS. TOPPED THE
> N.L. IN HITTING THREE TIMES, BATTING
> OVER .400 TO GAIN THE CHAMPIONSHIP
> IN 1895 AND 1896.

FRED CLARKE

Born on October 3, 1872, in Winterset, Iowa, Fred Clifford Clarke joined Louisville in the National League in 1894. He quit school after the sixth grade to bring in money to help support his family and wound up years later with a fortune estimated at over $2 million.

"Hayseed" was written all over Clarke when he reported to the team in 1894 carrying a straw suitcase and an undersized bat. Louisville manager Bill Barnie snapped: "Clarke, get yourself a uniform and suit up for the game."

"I was supposed to get a hundred for coming here," Clarke snapped back. "I want the money now before I do anything for the team."

Barnie obtained the $100 and gave it to Clarke.

In uniform, swinging the undersized bat, Clarke became a target for his new teammates. "The pitchers here will saw that damn kid's bat right out of your hand, rookie," they teased him. Clarke did not respond.

When the game was over and Clarke had recorded five hits, the first of his 2,703 lifetime hits, he smiled at those who had razzed him: "Those pitchers had a hell of a time knocking the bat out of my hands."

A left-handed-batting left fielder, Fred Clarke's fearless playing style was compared to that of Ty Cobb. He was no slouch as a player either, earning Hall of Fame election due to his career batting average of .312, base running (506 steals), and tremendous throwing arm. With the Pittsburgh Bucs, Clarke batted in front of Honus Wagner, forming one of the most feared duos in baseball in the early 20th century.

"A square deal for everybody. . . . Get results."

—Fred Clarke

Clarke was admitted to the Baseball Hall of Fame in 1945. His plaque reads:

FRED CLARKE
THE FIRST OF THE SUCCESSFUL
"BOY MANAGERS," AT TWENTY-FOUR HE
PILOTED LOUISVILLE'S COLONELS IN
THE NATIONAL LEAGUE. WON 4 PENNANTS
FOR PITTSBURGH AND A WORLD
CHAMPIONSHIP IN 1909. STARRED AS
AN OUTFIELDER FOR 22 SEASONS.

JOHN CLARKSON

Adrian "Cap" Anson had this to say of John Clarkson after his death in 1909:

> Clarkson was one of the greatest pitchers of all time, certainly the best Chicago ever had. Many regard him as the greatest, but not many know of his peculiar temperament and the amount of encouragement needed to keep him going.
>
> Scold him, find fault with him, and he could not, would not pitch at all. Praise him, and he was unbeatable. In knowing what kind of a ball a batter could not hit and his ability to serve up that kind of ball, I don't think I have ever seen the equal of Clarkson.

John Gibson Clarkson was a standout among 19th-century pitchers, a force powering Chicago to three straight pennants, winning 53 games in 1885, 35 in 1886, and 38 in 1887. He was a horse starter in an era of two-man rotations, pacing the National League in wins, appearances, starts, complete games, innings, and strikeouts in 1885, 1887, and 1889; in shutouts in 1885 and 1889; and in strikeouts and earned-run average (ERA) in 1889.

A popping fastball accounted for the handsome hurler's early success; when some of that pop was lost, he added a drop curveball and a change of pace, always adjusting. He used intimidation when he had to, staring at the batter from deep-set dark eyes, pitching in a paced and assured manner.

His National League career was spent with Worcester (1882), Chicago (1884–1887), Boston (1888–1892), and Cleveland (1892–1894) but was sadly cut short by his witnessing a horrible train accident involving his catcher and friend, Charley Bennett, who lost parts of both legs, and Clarkson becoming somewhat unbalanced. He pitched for just one season after that. When he retired from the game, Clarkson was the winningest pitcher in National League history.

Admitted to the Hall of Fame in 1963, his plaque reads:

JOHN GIBSON CLARKSON

WORCESTER, N.L. 1882

CHICAGO, N.L. 1884–87

BOSTON, N.L. 1888–92

CLEVELAND, N.L. 1892–94

PITCHED 4 TO 0 NO-HIT GAME AGAINST

PROVIDENCE IN 1885. WON 328 LOST 175

PCT .652 LED LEAGUE WITH 53 VICTORIES

IN 1885 (INCLUDING 10 SHUTOUTS) 38 IN

1887, 49 IN 1888 AND 49 IN 1889. HAD

2013 STRIKEOUTS IN 4514 INNINGS.

JIMMY COLLINS

Hall of Famer Jimmy Collins held down third base in the greatest infield in 19th-century baseball. His mates at Boston included Fred Tenney at first base, Bobby Lowe at second, and Herman Long at shortstop. It was Collins who totally revolutionized the way third basemen played their position. He was the first third baseman to play off the base, the first to play shallow and charge the ball, use his quick reflexes to spear the ball bare-handed, and fire it to first base.

Collins even made the skeptical Baltimore Orioles into believers. In one memorable game, John McGraw bunted. Collins charged, speared, and fired the ball to first base. McGraw was retired. Wee Willie Keeler bunted. Collins repeated his act. Keeler was retired. Four Orioles in succession attempted to bunt their way on. Four Orioles in a row were retired by Collins. They got the message and ceased bunting on him.

For five seasons with Boston, James Joseph Collins, a native of Buffalo, New York, averaged 300 or more assists a year. His lifetime batting average was .294, but it was the glove of Collins that was the biggest argument for his admission to baseball's Hall of Fame and his reputation as one of the top players in 19th-century baseball. His Hall of Fame admission came in 1945. His plaque reads:

> JAMES COLLINS
> CONSIDERED BY MANY THE GAME'S
> GREATEST THIRD BASEMAN. HE
> REVOLUTIONIZED STYLE OF PLAY AT THAT
> BAG. LED BOSTON RED SOX TO FIRST
> WORLD CHAMPIONSHIP IN 1903. A
> CONSISTENT BATTER, HIS DEFENSIVE PLAY
> THRILLED FANS OF BOTH MAJOR LEAGUES.

ROGER CONNOR

A powerfully built Irishman, Roger Connor began his playing career with Troy in the National League in 1880. He went on to become one of the first great power hitters in baseball, the home run king of the 19th century. Connor smashed 132 home runs from 1880 to 1897. He also ranks among the all-time career leaders in triples, with 227.

One of eight children of Irish immigrants in Waterbury, Connecticut, Connor sometimes ignored family chores to play baseball, to the chagrin of his hard-nosed parents who, like others of the time, felt baseball was not a respectable trade and would not allow Connor to engage in the sport.

Nevertheless, at the age of 14 Connor left home for New York City to play baseball. When he returned to Waterbury, his father had passed away. To help support the family, the youth worked in a local factory and played in neighborhood games of baseball. When Connor was about 21 years old, his mother gave him permission to play with the New Bedford team in Massachusetts.

The rise up the baseball ladder for the young man was amazing. After just 11 games for New Bedford in 1878, Connor moved on to Holyoke, where he hit .335. By 1880, he was with Troy City of the National League, where he hit .332. His 19th-century career was spent this way: Troy Trojans (1880–1882), New York Gothams/Giants

(1883–1889, 1891, 1893–1894), New York Giants–Players League (1890), Philadelphia Phillies (1892), St. Louis Browns (1894–1897).

It was during his time as a slugging first baseman for the New York Giants that his nickname "Dear Old Rog" was in the forefront. One of his most memorable home runs was hit out of the old Polo Grounds at 110th Street and Fifth Avenue in New York City. The ball made its way over the right field fence and finally came to rest on 112th Street. Fans gave Connor a $500 gold watch as a trophy commemorating the event.

Connor's most prolific day at the plate took place on June 1, 1895. He was then playing for the St. Louis Browns against his old team, the New York Giants. He went six for six.

Connor hit 10 or more home runs seven times (a 19th-century record), once hit three homers in one game (May 9, 1888), and was the first ballplayer to hit an over-the-wall home run at the Polo Grounds. He was also the first to hit a grand slam homer. That came on September 10, 1881, with two outs in the bottom of the ninth and his team trailing by three runs.

The slugging first baseman bested the .300 mark in each of 12 seasons. Durability was another resume line for the power-hitting superstar of the dead-ball era. He played in 1,083 of a possible 1,100 games from 1880 to 1889.

Hall of Fame admission came to Connor in 1976. His plaque reads:

ROGER CONNOR
TROY N.L., NEW YORK N.L.,
NEW YORK P.L., PHILADELPHIA N.L.,
ST. LOUIS N.L. 1880–1897
POWER–HITTING STAR OF DEAD–BALL ERA.
SET CAREER HOME RUN RECORD FOR 19TH
CENTURY PLAYERS. WON LEAGUE BATTING
CHAMPIONSHIP IN 1885 AND HIT .300 OR
BETTER 12 TIMES. HIT THREE HOMERS
IN A GAME IN 1888 AND MADE SIX HITS IN
SIX AT-BATS IN A GAME IN 1895.

CANDY CUMMINGS

As a young man strolling the beaches in Brooklyn in 1865, Arthur Cummings noticed that clamshells tossed underhand would curve to the right. In boarding school, Cummings played around with a baseball, and with a horizontal whip of the wrist was able to make the ball rise and drop. Thus was the curveball born. Actually, what Cummings did was to snap his wrist and the second finger of his right hand when releasing the ball, making it curve.

It was reported that he said: "A surge of joy flooded over me that I shall never forget. I felt like shouting out that I had made a ball curve. I wanted to tell everyone. It was too good to keep to myself."

His first highly publicized exhibition of what a curveball could do took place in 1867 when he was pressed into service as a member of the Excelsiors of Brooklyn, then playing against the Harvards of Cambridge. The curveball that Cummings threw, in the words of one Harvard player, "came at us and then went away from us." His "secret" curveball caused many a batter to throw down his bat in disgust and stalk away from the plate.

The curveball became widely imitated and the pitcher's best friend after others saw what Candy Cummings was able to accomplish. From 1868 to 1872 Cummings pitched for the Stars of Brooklyn, a group that called itself the "championship team of the United States and Canada." He then plied his trade with the Mutuals and other teams.

Unfortunately, by 1877, the 120-pound Cummings was through. His touch was gone. The legacy of Candy Cummings was the curveball—the pitch that changed the game and enabled its inventor to become a member of baseball's Hall of Fame, if one of the least-known members.

His nickname "Candy" was a term of endearment from fans who adored him and appreciated that he was of the best pitchers in the nation in the 1870s, pitching for the New York Mutuals (1872), Baltimore Lord Baltimores (1873), Philadelphia Whites (1874), Hartford Dark Blues (1875–1876), and Cincinnati Reds (1877). The name "Candy" was also a synonym for "the best" during the 19th century.

Although there has always been some dispute as to whether or not Candy Cummings invented the curveball, he mastered "the curve pitch" well before many others. And besides, his Hall of Fame plaque reads:

> W. A. "CANDY" CUMMINGS
> PITCHED FIRST CURVE BALL IN BASEBALL
> HISTORY. INVENTED CURVE AS AMATEUR
> ACE OF BROOKLYN STARS IN 1867.

ED DELAHANTY

One of five Irish brothers from Cleveland who excited the world of baseball around the turn of the century, Edward James Delahanty was the biggest and the best athlete of the quintet. His major league debut was on May 22, 1888, as a member of the Philadelphia Quakers. He played for them through 1888–1889, then it was on to the Cleveland Infants (1890), Philadelphia Phillies (1891–1901), and Washington Senators (1902–1903).

Delahanty was a remarkable performer and had some terrific marker moments: He had a six-hit game in 1890 and again in 1894. He stroked 10 consecutive hits in 1897. On a July afternoon in 1896 he became the second player in history to hammer four home runs in a game.

In a 16-year major league career, the "King of Batters" recorded 2,597 hits and a lifetime batting average of .346. Delahanty as a member of the Philadelphia Phillies batted .408 to lead the National League in hitting in 1899. Three years later he led the American League in hitting. That makes him the only one to win batting titles in both leagues.

Just one of eight players to bat .400 or better twice, Delahanty notched a .400 average in 1894. However that fabled figure was good enough only for fourth place in the batting race behind Hugh

Duffy, Tuck Turner, and Sam Thompson. Turner and Thompson were teammates of Big Ed on a Philadelphia team that collectively batted .349 for the season.

Success for the man they called "Big Ed" was there for all to see. But he had a terrible dark side. A gambler, a boozer, a depressed personality—he would sometimes lapse into talk about suicide. His mother would accompany him on road trips as a barrier to his taking his life.

Out of the blue, death came to him on July 2, 1903. He had been suspended by his Detroit team because of noncompliance with training rules. Leaving the club in Detroit, he took a train to New York, allegedly to link up as a player for the Giants. At International Bridge near Niagara Falls, as the story goes, the conductor booted him off the train for drunk and disorderly behavior. Staggering along the tracks in the dark, he fell down through an open drawbridge and was tragically swept away to his death. That is the "official story," but there was and still persists a theory of foul play.

His entire family—including his four baseball brothers—attended his funeral, and numerous friends from around the world of baseball paid their last respects. John McGraw served as a pallbearer.

In 1945 the Veterans Committee of the Hall of Fame selected several "old-timers" to recognize the early days of baseball. Ed Delahanty was in that group. His plaque reads:

ED DELAHANTY
ONE OF THE GAME'S GREATEST SLUGGERS.
LED NATIONAL LEAGUE HITTERS IN
1899 WITH AN AVERAGE OF .408 FOR
PHILADELPHIA; AMERICAN LEAGUE
BATTERS IN 1902 WITH A MARK OF .376
FOR WASHINGTON. MADE 6 HITS IN 6
TIMES AT BAT TWICE DURING CAREER
AND ONCE HIT 4 HOME RUNS IN A GAME.

HUGH DUFFY

Hugh Duffy was born in Cranston, Rhode Island, on November 26, 1866. His major league playing career began with Chicago in 1888 in the National League. He finished it in 1908 as a member of Providence in the Eastern League. In between, he played for the Chicago Pirates (1890), Boston Reds (1891), Boston Beaneaters (1892–1900), Milwaukee Brewers (1901), and Philadelphia Phillies (1904–1906).

Reportedly just 5 feet, 7 inches tall, Duffy had broad shoulders and powerful arms and a wallop in his bat. But Chicago's manger Cap Anson was never that impressed with Duffy.

"Where's the rest of you?" snapped the tough Anson when he first saw Duffy.

"That's all there is," was the reply. Duffy was with Chicago for just two seasons—another of the mistakes Anson never quite got over.

While the slick-fielding outfielder didn't catch Anson's eye—female fans all over baseball noticed the dapper dresser with the handsome visage.

Duffy's most sublime season was 1894; playing for the Boston Beaneaters, he batted .438—the highest season batting average in major league baseball history. In 124 games, the player they called "Sir Hugh" managed 236 hits. In only 17 games did he fail to hit safely. Twice he stroked five hits in a game, and 12 times he rapped out four hits. "No one thought that much of averages in those days," Duffy recalled with a smile. "I didn't realize I had hit that much until the official averages were published four months later."

"Rewarded" for his accomplishment, Duffy had his salary jacked up $12.50 a week, increasing his annual wage to $2,750.

Hugh Duffy earned his place in the Hall of Fame as one of the best players of the 1890s. For that decade, he played more games, hit more homers, and drove in more runs than any other player in baseball.

Under contract in baseball for an amazing 68 years as player, manager, executive, coach, and team owner, part of Duffy's legacy was a stint in the 1930s as a coach for the Boston Red Sox. He schooled young players like Bobby Doerr and Ted Williams.

Duffy was admitted to the Baseball Hall of Fame in 1945. His plaque reads:

> HUGH DUFFY
> BRILLIANT AS A DEFENSIVE OUTFIELDER
> FOR THE BOSTON NATIONALS, HE
> COMPILED A BATTING AVERAGE IN 1894
> WHICH WAS NOT TO BE CHALLENGED
> IN HIS LIFETIME—.438.

BUCK EWING

His nickname "Buck" came from a hunting triumph when he was a teenager. Buck Ewing was known also as "Bread and Butter" because of his clutch qualities on the baseball field.

Acknowledged as the first catcher to crouch behind the plate, William "Buck" Ewing was the dominant backstop of 19th-century baseball, perhaps the greatest catcher of his era. John B. Foster, editor of the *Spalding Baseball Guide*, observed of the man who was the star catcher for the New York National League team of the 1880s:

> Buck could throw from any position. It was not by accident that he could throw fearlessly and unswervingly when he squatted down behind the batter, but he chose to throw that way, because he knew he could and did catch runners with the same easy skill that he would have caught them if he were standing.

The sharp snap of the forearm Ewing utilized to launch the ball to his fielders enabled them to catch base runners off guard. On the bases, Ewing turned the tables, recording impressive stolen base totals for himself. He didn't really have much speed, but studied opposing pitchers and knew when to make his move. Once he stole second and third base and shouted: "Now I'm stealing home"—and did what he claimed he would. That play was memorialized on a lithograph that was treasured by New York City sports fans of the time.

He may have been the most versatile player and best all-around player of the 19th century, since he played more than 200 games at catcher, first base, outfield, and third base. He won a home run title and finished in the top 10 in batting and slugging a combined 15 times. His versatility extended to the fact that he was credited with laying out the design of New York City's Polo Grounds.

Ewing's career spanned time with the Troy Trojans (1880–1882); New York Gothams, Mutuals, and Giants (1883–1889, 1891–1892); New York Giants–Players League (1890); Cleveland Spiders (1893–1894); and Cincinnati Reds (1895–1897).

Ewing batted .303 and stole 336 bases in an 18-year career that ended in 1897. He was admitted to baseball's Hall of Fame in 1939. His plaque reads:

> WM. B. "BUCK" EWING
> GREATEST 19TH CENTURY CATCHER. GIANT
> IN STATURE AND GIANT CAPTAIN OF
> NEW YORK'S FIRST NATIONAL LEAGUE
> CHAMPIONS 1888 AND 1889. WAS GENIUS
> AS FIELD LEADER, UNSURPASSED IN
> THROWING TO BASES, GREAT LONG-RANGE
> HITTER. NATIONAL LEAGUE CAREER
> 1881 TO 1899 TROY, N.Y. GIANTS AND
> CLEVELAND; CINCINNATI MANAGER.

PUD GALVIN

In the all-time top 10 in wins, losses, complete games, games started, and shutouts, Pud Galvin was the Walter Johnson of his time, 1879 to 1892. Known as "Gentle Jeems" and the "Little Steam Engine," the 5-foot, 8-inch, 190-pound right-hander was paid this tribute by Buck Ewing: "If I had Galvin to catch, no one would ever steal a base on me. That fellow keeps 'em glued to the bases and also has the best control of any pitcher in the league."

Pure power and control made the stocky Galvin a master practitioner of pitching excellence. He won 46 games, working the staggering total of 656 innings in 1883. In 1884 he again won 46 games. His 5,959 lifetime innings pitched is more than any other hurler in baseball history except for Cy Young.

Galvin was 37–27 for Buffalo in 1879, his rookie season. It was first of six straight 20-win seasons for him. His most triumphant years were with Buffalo, where during a six-day period in 1884 he hurled a one-hitter, then a three-hitter, and then a third game of 11 innings of shutout ball.

Ironically, with all of his storied pitching accomplishments, it was not until 63 years after his death that James Francis Galvin was finally admitted to baseball's Hall of Fame in 1965. His plaque reads:

JAMES F. (PUD) GALVIN
ST. LOUIS N.A. 1875
BUFFALO N.L. 1879–1885
PITTSBURGH A.A. 1885–1886
PITTSBURGH N.L. 1887–1889 1891–1892
PITTSBURGH P.L. 1890
ST. LOUIS N.L. 1892
WON 365 GAMES. LOST 311.
WHEN ELECTED ONLY FOUR PITCHERS
HAD WON MORE GAMES.
PITCHED NO-HIT GAMES IN 1880 AND 1884.
PITCHED 649 COMPLETE GAMES.

CLARK GRIFFITH

Born on November 20, 1869, in Stringtown, Missouri, Clark Calvin Griffith is best known as a manager and an owner, but he was also one of the top pitchers for Cap Anson's Chicago team in the 1890s.

Dubbed the "Old Fox" because of his thinking approach to pitching, Griffith had many battles with John McGraw. Once the old Baltimore Oriole singled and was on first base taunting Griffith. The umpire suggested that Griffith pick off McGraw, but with the small lead the arrogant Oriole was assuming it was not a feasible tactic.

"Balk him off," the umpire suggested.

Griffith followed orders, purposely balking to first base. No balk was called by the umpire. McGraw protested so vociferously that he was thrown out of the game by the umpire.

Griffith attempted the same technique with the next batter, who reached first base safely. It was to no avail. "Balks work only with McGraw," the ump explained.

Griffith, however, didn't really have to resort to chicanery—his talent was enough to reel off six straight 20-win seasons in the 1890s. His playing career was spent with St. Louis Browns (1891), Boston Reds (1891), Chicago Colts/Orphans (1893–1900), Chicago White Sox (1901–1902), New York Highlanders (1903–1907), Cincinnati Reds (1909), and Washington Senators (1912–1914).

He was admitted to the Baseball Hall of Fame in 1946. His plaque reads:

CLARK C. GRIFFITH

ASSOCIATED WITH MAJOR LEAGUE BASEBALL
FOR MORE THAN 50 YEARS AS A PITCHER,
MANAGER AND EXECUTIVE. SERVED AS A
MEMBER OF THE CHICAGO AND CINCINNATI
TEAMS IN THE N.L. AND THE CHICAGO,
NEW YORK AND WASHINGTON CLUBS
IN THE A.L. COMPILED MORE THAN 200
VICTORIES AS A PITCHER. MANAGER OF THE
CINCINNATI N.L. AND CHICAGO, NEW YORK
AND WASHINGTON A.L. TEAMS FOR 20 YEARS.

BILLY HAMILTON

Stocky Billy Hamilton made his major league debut on July 31, 1888. He played from that year until 1901, and in that time stole 912 bases. Three years in a row he stole over a hundred bases. His steals and his slides earned him his nickname "Sliding Billy." His exploits on the base paths and a .344 lifetime batting average were more than good enough to get him admitted to baseball's Hall of Fame.

The 1894 season was just one of the zeniths of Hamilton's career. He scored 196 runs in 131 games, batted .399, and stole seven bases in one game.

The Newark, New Jersey, lad was a former high school sprinter. He played for the Kansas City Cowboys (1888–1889), Philadelphia Phillies (1890–1895), and Boston Beaneaters (1896–1901).

"Sliding Billy" is one of only three players in big league history with more runs scored than games played. Hamilton was perhaps the best player of the 1890s. Seven times a stolen-base champion, he combined raw speed, daring base running, and patience at the plate, becoming the game's first great leadoff hitter.

He was a true baseball revolutionary in that he made the head-first slide, the first-to-third advance on a base hit, and the drag bunt staples of the 1890s game. In spite of all he accomplished, Hamilton was not admitted to the Baseball Hall of Fame until 1961—21 years after his death and 60 years after he played his final game.

For much of Hamilton's career, a stolen base was awarded when a base runner advanced an extra base on a hit, so a first-to-third advancement on a single was one stolen base for the lead runner. This rule was changed in 1898 to the present definition of a stolen base.

His Hall of fame plaque reads:

> WILLIAM R. HAMILTON
> PHILADELPHIA N.L. 1890–1895
> BOSTON N.L. 1896–1901
> HOLDS RECORDS FOR SINGLE SEASON:
> RUNS SCORED, 196 IN 1894; STOLEN
> BASES, 115 IN 1891. LIFETIME TOTAL
> STOLEN BASES, 937. BATTED .395 IN
> 1893, .399 IN 1894, .393 IN 1895.
> LED NATIONAL LEAGUE IN 1891 WITH
> .338 AVERAGE. LIFETIME BATTING
> AVERAGE OF .344. SCORED 100 OR
> MORE RUNS DURING 10 SEASONS.

HUGHIE JENNINGS

Born April 2, 1869, in Pittston, Pennsylvania, freckle-faced, 5-foot, 8-inch Hugh Ambrose Jennings joined the Baltimore Orioles of John J. McGraw, Wee Willie Keeler, Dan Brouthers, Wilbert Robinson, and Joe Kelley—all future Hall of Famers—in 1894. Jennings learned a lot from being in such an exceptional environment for the honing of baseball skills.

A skillful and speedy base runner, Jennings was also a fine fielding shortstop. Five times he led the National League in fielding. "Hughie Jennings," said Honus Wagner, "was the first shortstop never to leave his position until the hitter either hit the ball or missed it. He had wonderful reflexes." The legendary Wagner also acknowledged a personal debt to Jennings, claiming that he modeled much of his defensive approach after that of the tough Baltimore Orioles shortstop.

Jennings was both a survivor and an intellect. Three times he came back from skull fractures. Once he was near death from a fastball thrown by pitcher Amos Rusie that smashed into his head. Another time he survived a running dive into a concrete swimming pool that had been unexpectedly drained. And there was the time that his car went over the side of a mountain.

The Orioles boasted six Hall of Famers in their everyday lineup: Robinson behind the plate, Brouthers at first, McGraw at third, Jennings at shortstop, Kelley in center field, and Keeler in right field. They won the National League pennant in 1894, 1895, and 1896. In 1897 and 1898 they finished a close second. In 1899, when Hanlon jumped to the Brooklyn team, Jennings, Kelley, and Keller went with him and the quartet won two more pennants, in 1899 and 1900. In all, Jennings's playing career saw him with stops with the Louisville Colonels, Baltimore Orioles, Brooklyn Superbas, Philadelphia Phillies, and Detroit Tigers.

The ambitious and intellectual Jennings bartered his way to a law degree by coaching the Cornell baseball team in return for tuition remission. He went on to become one of baseball's greatest managers.

Jennings may be one of the most misunderstood Hall of Fame members. He was elected as a shortstop, but there are those who state he was elected because of his 16-year managerial career, where he piloted 1,131 games. Elected to the Hall of Fame by the Committee on Baseball Veterans in 1945, his plaque reads:

HUGHIE JENNINGS
OF BALTIMORE'S FAMOUS OLD ORIOLES,
HE WAS ONE OF THE GAME'S MIGHTY
MITES. A STAR SHORTSTOP HE WAS A
CONSTANT THREAT AT THE PLATE.
ONCE HIT .397. PILOTED DETROIT
TO THREE CHAMPIONSHIPS.

TIM KEEFE

The son of Irish immigrants, Tim Keefe was a mainstay of the New York Giants from 1885 to 1889. Keefe was a gentle and soft-spoken man and was given the affectionate nicknames "Sir Timothy" and "Smiling Tim." The well-built right-hander ranks in the all-time top 10 in wins, complete games, and innings pitched. Keefe possessed a good fastball and curve, but his change of pace so effectively complemented his other pitches that it was his complete repertoire that made him an outstanding hurler.

His sensitivity was reflected in an 1887 incident. One of his fastballs struck Boston second baseman John Burdock on the temple. Keefe was so unsettled by what he had done that he suffered a nervous breakdown, missing a few weeks of the season. After the season, Keefe entered a sanitarium during the winter—that's how much hitting Burdock and a few other batters in the 1887 season had affected him.

After his incredible 1888 season—35 wins, 12 losses, a 1.74 ERA, and 333 strikeouts— Keefe was signed to a contract of $4,500 a year, making him the highest-paid player on the New York Giants.

An odd footnote to Keefe's career was that his rookie season of 1880 was the last time pitchers delivered the ball from 45 feet, and his last season of 1893 was the first where hurlers threw from 60 feet, 6 inches.

Hall of Fame admission came for the smiling Irishman in 1964. His Hall of Fame plaque reads:

TIMOTHY J. KEEFE
1880–1893
RIGHTHANDER WHO WON 346 GAMES
FOR TROY, METS, GIANTS AND PHILS
IN ONLY 14 SEASONS.
HIS RECORD STREAK OF 19 STRAIGHT TRIUMPHS
PACED GIANTS TO FLAG IN 1888.
ONE OF FIRST PITCHERS
TO USE A CHANGE OF PACE DELIVERY.

"WEE WILLIE" KEELER

The man who would later be known as "Wee" Willie Keeler made his debut at the Polo Grounds as a member of the New York Giants on September 30, 1892. He singled off the Phillies' Tim Keefe for the first of his 2,926 career hits.

Two years later Keeler became a member of the famed Baltimore Orioles. Batting at the top of the lineup for Ned Hanlon, the little man was a member of the 1890s Orioles teams that revolutionized the way baseball was played. Keeler was skillful at laying down bunts, chopping the ball into the ground and beating it out for an infield hit, and executing the suicide squeeze.

The son of a Brooklyn trolley switchman, just 5-foot-4 and 140 pounds, the left-handed-hitting Keeler more than made up for his lack of size with fine running speed and deft bat control. His bat was the shortest in the history of major league baseball at 30.5 inches.

Keeler opened the 1897 season with two hits in five at-bats against Boston. Then for two months the slight southpaw swinger slapped hit after hit, game after game—from April 22 to June 18—for 44 straight games. His record stood for 44 years until Joe DiMaggio came along and snapped it in 1941.

That 1897 season, Keeler batted an incredible .432. A reporter asked the diminutive batter, "Mr. Keeler, how can a man your size hit .432?"

The reply to that question has become a rallying cry for all kinds of baseball players in all kinds of leagues: "Simple," Keeler smiled. "I keep my eyes clear and I hit 'em where they ain't." That he did.

The *Sporting News* offered this mangled prose about Keeler as a fielder:

> He swears by the teeth of his mask-carved horse chestnut, that he always carries with him as a talisman that he inevitably dreams of it in the night before when he is going to boot one—muff an easy fly ball, that is to say, in the meadow on the morrow. "All of us fellows in the outworks have got just so many of them in a season to drop and there's no use trying to buck against fate."

In 1898, Keeler set a mark for hitting that will probably never be topped, notching 202 singles in just 128 games. He truly was hitting them where the fielders weren't. It was a season in which the left-handed bat magician recorded 214 hits. His batting average was .379, but the incredible amount of singles amassed saw him register a puny .410 slugging percentage. That 1898 season, Keeler came to bat 564 times in 128 games and walked only 28 times and did not strike out.

In 1899, Keeler returned to his place of birth and was a member of the Brooklyn team, which won pennants that year and the next. Thus, in his first seven seasons as a regular player, Keeler's teams won five pennants and twice finished second. With him in the lineup, clubs scored a lot of runs. The little man's .345 lifetime batting average ranks him fifth on the all-time list.

His playing career in right field of 2,013 games included these stops: New York Giants (1892–1893, 1910), Brooklyn Grooms (1893), Baltimore Orioles (1894–1898), Brooklyn Superbas (1899–1902), New York Highlanders (1903–1909). He never played in the minors.

Ogden Nash even devoted some poetry to him:

> K is for Keeler
> As fresh as green paint
> The fustest and mostest
> To hit where they ain't.

Hall of Fame admission came for Keeler with the first class in 1939. His plaque reads:

WILLIE KEELER
"HIT 'EM WHERE THEY AINT!"
BASEBALL'S GREATEST PLACE-HITTER;
BEST BUNTER. BIG LEAGUE CAREER
1892 TO 1910 WITH N.Y. GIANTS,
BALTIMORE ORIOLES, BROOKLYN SUPERBAS,
N.Y. HIGHLANDERS. NATIONAL LEAGUE
BATTING CHAMPION '97–'98.

JOE KELLEY

Joseph James Kelley made his debut on July 27, 1891—he singled in his first at-bat off future Hall of Fame pitcher Mickey Welch. That was how he started and he never let up.

Since the Baltimore Orioles were one of the most dominant teams of 19th-century baseball, it is no surprise that many of the dominant players performed for the O's. Joe Kelley was not only a dominant player, he was also one of the most unusual.

One of his props was a mirror that he kept in his pocket and from time to time used as he stood out in left field waiting for some action. The mirror was useful for Kelley, enabling him to primp and pamper his ample face more effectively.

Kelley was always active in left field, sometimes burying balls in the tall grass—little decoys at the ready, available for Kelley's employment when the right moment came along.

From 1893 on, Kelley batted over .300 for a dozen straight seasons. One of his greatest campaigns was 1894, when he batted .391 and stole 45 bases. And on September 3 of that year, he managed a record nine hits in nine at-bats in a doubleheader—three singles and a triple in the first game, four doubles and a single in the second game.

Energetic, attractive, and talented, Joseph James Kelley, a native of Cambridge, Massachusetts, was one of the most popular players of his time. He was enshrined in the Baseball Hall of Fame in 1971. His Hall of Fame plaque reads:

JOSEPH JAMES KELLEY, 1891–1908
STANDOUT HITTER AND LEFT FIELDER OF
CHAMPION 1894–95–96 BALTIMORE ORIOLES
AND 1899–1900 BROOKLYN SUPERBAS. BATTED
OVER .300 FOR 11 CONSECUTIVE YEARS WITH
HIGH OF .391 IN 1894. EQUALLED RECORD
WITH 9 HITS IN 9 AT-BATS IN DOUBLEHEADER.
ALSO PLAYED FOR BOSTON, PITTSBURGH AND
CINCINNATI OF N.L. AND BALTIMORE OF A.L.
MANAGED CINCINNATI 1902 TO 1905 AND
BOSTON N.L. IN 1908.

KING KELLY

As a teenager, Michael Joseph Kelly began his baseball career playing for the Patterson (New Jersey) Keystones. The word was that he could hit harder, throw farther, and run faster than anyone on the team. His first professional stop was with the Cincinnati Reds and then on to the White Stockings of Chicago in 1879. Stealing bases was his specialty now—he once pilfered six bases in a game. In 1887, the second year stolen base records were kept, the likable athlete stole a total of 84 during the season. That inspired the popular song "Slide, Kelley, Slide" and made "King Kel" one of the first great superstars in baseball history.

"King Kel" could outdo any man moving from base to base or bar to bar. A 5-foot-10 185-pounder, Michael Joseph Kelly played primarily with the Chicago White Stockings. Chicago shocked the baseball world by selling Kelly to Boston in 1887 for the then unheard-of sum of $10,000. A lover of liquor, racehorses, and baseball, Kelly was an incredible and opportunistic competitor. Once he reportedly capitalized on a rule that enabled a substitute to enter a game at any time. As the batter swung at the ball, Kelly jumped off the dugout bench and screamed: "Kelly now catching." Then he smothered a foul pop-up that his team's regular catcher would never have reached.

Another time, in the bottom of the 12th inning, Kelly raced after a rising line drive. Leaping up in the distant recesses of the outfield, Kelly stuck his glove into the air and came trotting into the infield, ball in hand. The catch saved the game and his teammates were jubilant. "Nice catch, Kel," one of them shouted. "Not at all, not at all!" Kelly winked. "'Twent a mile above my head."

The lively Irishman never feared to differ with other's opinions—even a private detective's report of his after-hours activity. "In that place," he told manager Cap Anson, "where the detective reports me as taking a lemonade at three A.M.—he's wrong. I never drank a lemonade at that hour in me life. It was straight whiskey."

Kelly's daring base stealing and opportunistic play made the refrain "slide, Kelly, slide," symbolize to multitudes just how exciting baseball could be. Once a laborer for three dollars a week in a paper mill, he earned $4,000 a season in the years 1887–1889. And he added to that income with stage appearances during the off-season telling baseball stories in vaudeville houses and reciting "Casey at the Bat." He was even an author of sorts, lending his name to *Play Ball*, a book that sold for 25 cents and was dedicated to the baseball players and fans of the United States.

His last major league season was 1893, when he was 35 years old. It was then that Kelly's longtime ambition to play for a New York team was realized—but only for a short while. All the years of neglect had caught up with him. Much overweight, his drinking worsened, and his playing was subpar. His major league career ended—after playing in just a few games he was cut loose.

The following year he developed pneumonia. While he was being carried on a stretcher into Boston hospital, his bearers stumbled. Kelly fell to the floor. "That's my last slide," he joked.

On November 8, 1894, King Kelly, whom Cap Anson once had characterized as "great a hitter as anyone," died at the age of 36. In 1945 the Veterans Committee of the Hall of Fame selected several "old-timers" to recognize the early days of baseball. King Kelly was in that group. His Hall of Fame plaque reads:

MIKE J. (KING) KELLY
COLORFUL PLAYER AND AUDACIOUS
BASE-RUNNER. IN 1887 FOR BOSTON
HE HIT .394 AND STOLE 84 BASES.
HIS SALE FOR $10,000 WAS ONE OF
THE BIGGEST DEALS OF BASEBALL'S
EARLY HISTORY.

JOHN MCGRAW

John J. "Mugsy" McGraw was born on April 7, 1873, in tiny Truxton, New York, one of nine children of a father who was a $9-a-week railroad man. When John McGraw was 12 years old, his mother, stepsister, and three brothers died of diphtheria. In 1891, shaped by hard times and tragedy, after stops in various minor league cities like Olean, New York; Ocala, Florida; and Cedar Rapids, Iowa, the 5-foot, 7-inch, 155-pound youth joined the Baltimore Orioles.

He became the toughest player on what many deem the toughest team of all time. Primarily a third baseman, the young McGraw earned the nickname "Muggsy" because of his battling nature. Later when he became a manager, the nickname was "Little Napoleon."

> "The only popularity I know is to win."
>
> —John McGraw

The force behind three Baltimore pennants in the 1890s, McGraw batted well over .300 from 1893 to 1900. Expert at the hit-and-run play, the feisty infielder knew all the tricks of the game. He would tag at a runner's shirt, belt, or pants—slowing him down. He would spike and bully umpires and rile up crowds. He turned the hit-and-run play into his own personal weapon. He would foul off pitches with an ease that exasperated opponents—in that era, foul balls were not deemed strikes. Once he fouled 15 pitches in a row off Clark Griffith.

Feared, hated, criticized by the opposition, McGraw played on in his own ferocious style year after year, taking and giving no quarter. "I have been trying to play ball," he defended his approach, "for all there was in me to help my club win games. This I will continue to do."

His baseball stops as a player included Baltimore Orioles NL (1891–1899), St. Louis Cardinals (1900), Baltimore Orioles AL (1901–1902), and New York Giants (1902–1906). He managed the Baltimore Orioles NL (1899), Baltimore Orioles AL (1901–1902), and New York Giants (1902–1932). He was a tough old bird even when he was young.

McGraw had one of the keenest batting eyes of his era. He walked more than 100 times in three seasons, scored over 100 runs five times, batted .320 or higher each year from 1893 on, and also posted an on-base percentage of .400 or higher in every year from 1893 on, including a career-high mark of .547 in 1899.

His Hall of Fame admission came in 1937. His plaque reads:

JOHN J. MCGRAW

STAR THIRD BASEMAN OF THE

GREAT BALTIMORE ORIOLES, NATIONAL

LEAGUE CHAMPIONS IN THE '90's. FOR

30 YEARS MANAGER OF THE NEW YORK

GIANTS STARTING IN 1902.

UNDER HIS LEADERSHIP THE

GIANTS WON 10 PENNANTS AND 3

WORLD CHAMPIONSHIPS.

JOHN ALEXANDER "KING BID" MCPHEE

Born November 1, 1859, in Massena, New York, the slightly built McPhee played for the Cincinnati Red Stockings and Cincinnati Reds. He is considered by many to be the greatest second baseman of the 19th century.

Bid McPhee was an adept leadoff man and superior second baseman, despite playing bare-handed for the majority of his 18-year big league career. The last second baseman to play gloveless, he toughened up the skin on his hands by soaking them in salt water. He was a consistent league leader in double plays, fielding average, assists, and putouts. McPhee batted .300 or better on four occasions, topping the 100-run mark 10 times. He batted .281 for his career. His nickname "King Bid" was well deserved.

McPhee witnessed tremendous changes in baseball: when he made his debut in organized ball, pitchers threw underhand from 45 feet. It took seven balls to be awarded a walk. Overhand pitching for the next nine seasons, and the modern distance of 60' 6" from the pitcher's mound to home plate were other innovations he had to adjust to.

The future Hall of Famer just went about his business—always in condition, without flair, with a remarkable consistency reflecting the sober and sedate man that he was. He was never fined or ejected from a game. He was admitted to the Hall of Fame in 2000 by the Committee on Baseball Veterans. His plaque reads:

JOHN ALEXANDER MCPHEE

"BID"

CINCINNATI, A.A., 1882–89

CINCINNATI, N.L., 1890–99

ONE OF THE 19TH CENTURY'S PREMIER SECOND BASEMEN, HE WAS A STANDOUT FIELDER DESPITE PLAYING BAREHANDED FOR MOST OF HIS 18-YEAR CAREER. THE LAST SECOND BASEMAN TO PLAY WITHOUT A GLOVE, HE REGULARLY LED THE LEAGUE IN DOUBLE PLAYS, FIELDING AVERAGE, ASSISTS AND PUTOUTS. PLAYING WITH A GLOVE FOR THE FIRST TIME IN 1896, HIS FIELDING AVERAGE WAS .982, A MARK THAT STOOD FOR 29 YEARS. A SKILLED LEADOFF HITTER, HE COM-PILED 2,250 HITS AND TOPPED THE 100-RUN MARK 10 TIMES, INCLUDING A CAREER-BEST 139 IN 1886. KNOWN FOR HIS SOBER DISPOSITION AND EXEMPLARY SPORTSMANSHIP.

KID NICHOLS

Seventh on the all-time list of most wins by a pitcher, fourth in games started, and seventh in innings pitched, Charles Augustus

("Kid") Nichols starred for Boston in the last decade of the 19th century, winning 25 or more games for five straight seasons.

One of the legendary workhorse pitchers, Nichols hurled more than 400 innings a year in each of his first five major league seasons. He was always ready to relieve on days he didn't start games. A remarkable feature of his career was his finishing 531 of the 561 games he started. The Kid posted records of 30–11 and 29–12 in 1897 and 1898, leading the Boston Beaneaters to pennants both seasons.

At 5 feet, 10 inches and 180 pounds, the solidly built Nichols delivered a moving fastball, a major reason for his success on the mound. He got by with one of the strongest arms around—never really developing an off-speed pitch, just going with the fastball.

Ranked as one of the top five pitchers of his era, Nichols was the youngest pitcher to win 300 major league games. His career was spent with the Boston Beaneaters (1890–1901), St. Louis Cardinals (1904–1905), and Philadelphia Phillies (1905–1906).

In 1949, Nichols was admitted to baseball's Hall of Fame. His plaque reads:

CHARLES A. (KID) NICHOLS
RIGHT HANDED PITCHER WHO WON 30 OR
MORE GAMES FOR SEVEN CONSECUTIVE
YEARS (1891–97) AND WON AT LEAST 20
GAMES FOR TEN CONSECUTIVE SEASONS
(1890–99) WITH BOSTON N.L. ALSO PITCHED
FOR ST. LOUIS AND PHILADELPHIA N.L. ONE
OF FEW PITCHERS TO WIN MORE THAN 300
GAMES, HIS MAJOR LEAGUE RECORD BEING
360 VICTORIES, 202 DEFEATS.

JIM O'ROURKE

James Henry O'Rourke began his pro career in 1872 with the Middletown Mansfields. He had the good fortune to be on six pennant-winning clubs in seven years, from 1873 to 1879. He recorded the first hit in major league history. In 1876, as a member of the Boston team, O'Rourke singled to left field with two outs in the first inning off Philadelphia's Lon Knight.

Dubbed "Orator Jim" because of his way with words, O'Rourke began his major league baseball career with Boston in 1873 in the National Association. It was there that manager Harry Wright suggested he change his name to "Mr. Wright" to conceal his Irish origins—at that time the Irish were not very popular in Boston. O'Rourke flashed the language that earned him his nickname: "I would rather die than give up my father's name. A million dollars would not tempt me."

In 1879, O'Rourke, playing for the Boston Red Caps, led all hitters with a .521 slugging average and 62 RBIs. One of the most popular players of his time, O'Rourke's lifetime batting average was .310.

In 1945, "Orator Jim" was inducted into the Hall of Fame. His plaque reads:

JAMES H. O'ROURKE

"ORATOR JIM" PLAYED BALL UNTIL HE
WAS PAST FIFTY, INCLUDING TWENTY-ONE
MAJOR LEAGUE SEASONS. AN OUTFIELDER
AND CATCHER FOR THE BOSTON RED
STOCKINGS OF 1873, HE LATER WORE
THE UNIFORMS OF THE CHAMPIONSHIP
PROVIDENCE TEAM OF 1879, BUFFALO,
NEW YORK AND WASHINGTON.

CHARLEY RADBOURN

A sturdy right-hander who developed his pitching skill on his family farm, the man they called "Old Hoss," Charles Radbourn, piled up extraordinary pitching endurance records in the years 1881–1891. His specialty was hurling complete games—489 of them in his career, placing him seventh on the all-time list.

In 1883, Radbourn tossed an 8–0 no-hitter against the Cleveland Blues on July 25. Radbourn was one of the most dominant pitchers of his day, winning 31 in 1882, 49 in 1883, and an incredible 60 in 1884 (including 26 out of the final 27). That 1884 season was his high-water mark. The Rochester, New York, native racked up a 60–12 record (the most wins by any pitcher ever in one season), striking out 411 batters in 679 innings as a member of Providence. In a stretch between August 7 and September 6, the Grays won 20 games in a row—and, astonishingly, all but two of the victories were accounted for by Radbourn. His salary for that momentous season performance was a meager $3,000.

One of his more unusual pitching days took place on September 13, 1889. He pitched a complete doubleheader for Boston, but failed to win either game. Losing the opener to Cleveland, 3–0, he had to hammer a home run in the ninth inning of the nightcap and salvage a 4–4 tie.

Radbourn paid a hefty price for his professional hurling heroics. There were times when he was totally unable to raise his pitching arm above his ear. In Radbourn's time, players as a matter of course were their own trainers and healers, and the powerful pitcher had his own patented routine. Hot towels applied in relays to his abused muscles eased his pain. An iron ball flipped underhand by Radbourn was phase two of his special treatment. Then he would throw a baseball from three or four times the regulation pitching distance before a game, until he finally was ready to pitch again.

Radbourn's career was spent with the Providence Grays, Boston Beaneaters, Boston Reds, and Cincinnati Reds. His admission to the

Baseball Hall of Fame came in 1939. His plaque (which spells his last name with an "e," and uses "Charlie") reads:

> CHARLIE RADBOURNE
> "OLD HOSS"
> PROVIDENCE, BOSTON AND CINCINNATI
> NATIONAL LEAGUE 1881 TO 1891. GREATEST
> OF ALL 19TH CENTURY PITCHERS. WINNING
> 1884 PENNANT FOR PROVIDENCE, RADBOURNE
> PITCHED LAST 27 GAMES OF SEASON, WON
> 26. WON 3 STRAIGHT IN WORLD SERIES.

WILBERT ROBINSON

Born the son of a butcher on June 2, 1863, in Bolton, Massachusetts, Wilbert Robinson's image and reputation in baseball legend and lore derive from his deeds and misdeeds as a manager of some madcap Brooklyn teams. He was a piece of work.

However, he was a fine baseball player—especially as a member of the Baltimore Orioles from 1892 to 1899. On June 10, 1892, Robby came to bat seven times and recorded seven hits. He also batted in 11 runs as Baltimore romped over St. Louis, 25–4. The daily newspapers the following day failed to make note of what Robinson had accomplished. It wasn't until two decades later that the famed sportswriter Heywood Broun publicized the event. The legendary scribe learned about it in an offhand conversation with Robby.

The burly Robinson was the team captain of the Orioles. Never a potent hitter, his prime value to the team was as an excellent handler of pitchers and as a defensive, durable catcher. His left "meat" hand had each finger broken at least once. His pinky finger's tip was amputated to stop blood poisoning from spreading to the rest of his body.

> "Don't worry about it fellows. I'm an old Oriole. I'm too tough to die."
>
> —Wilbert Robinson

Robinson was admitted to the Baseball Hall of Fame in 1945. His plaque reads:

WILBERT ROBINSON
"UNCLE ROBBIE"
STAR CATCHER FOR THE FAMOUS
BALTIMORE ORIOLES ON PENNANT CLUBS
OF 1894, '95 AND '96. HE LATER WON FAME
AS MANAGER OF THE BROOKLYN DODGERS
FROM 1914 THROUGH 1931. SET A RECORD OF
7 HITS IN 7 TIMES AT BAT IN SINGLE GAME.

AMOS RUSIE

New York City baseball fans have thrilled to the deeds of many top athletes; however, the first great sports hero in the Big Apple was the big farmer from Moorseville, Indiana, they called the "Hoosier Thunderbolt," Amos Rusie. He personified sheer power pitching in the 1890s.

Amos Rusie was the principal reason the pitcher's mound was moved back from 50 feet to the present 60 feet, 6 inches in 1893. Ironically, the change in distance, though it created more safety for batters, also increased success for Rusie, who was able to have more yardage for his breaking curveball.

Rusie had many baseball skills. As a pitcher, he had a good breaking curveball and an effective change of pace. He hit well and played outfield on an occasional day off from the mound.

A powerful right-handed pitcher, Rusie's speed and wildness were the stuff of legends. Five times he led the National League in walks, placing him fifth on the all-time list in that category. One of his high hard ones rendered Baltimore shortstop Hughie Jennings unconscious for almost four days. Another fastball came roaring back at Rusie off the bat of a hitter, smashed into the pitcher's ear, and caused him permanent hearing damage.

In 1890, he came to the New York Giants, after a season with his hometown Indianapolis team, to fill a hole when several Giants defected to the Players League. In their absence he had led the league with 36 wins and in winning percentage and strikeouts.

From 1890 to 1898, as a New York Giant, Rusie had his greatest success. He won more than 20 games a season—except for 1896: He did not perform that season protesting what he called "unjust fines" levied in 1895. The 1897 season, the best of his career, saw his line as 29 wins, 8 losses, best ERA. He won 30 or more games four times (1891–1894), struck out 300 or more batters twice (1890 and 1891), and was the league leader in strikeouts five times (1890–1891, 1893–1895). He also regularly posted an ERA below 3.00. On December 15, 1900, he was traded by the New York Giants to the Cincinnati Reds for Christy Mathewson.

Rusie was admitted to the Baseball Hall of Fame in 1977. His plaque reads:

AMOS WILSON RUSIE
"THE HOOSIER THUNDERBOLT"
INDIANAPOLIS N.L., NEW YORK N.L.,
CINCINNATI N.L., 1889–1895 1897–1898 AND 1901
GENERALLY CONSIDERED FIREBALL KING OF
NINETEENTH-CENTURY MOUNDSMEN. NOTCHED
BETTER THAN 240 VICTORIES IN TEN-YEAR
CAREER. ACHIEVED 30-VICTORY MARK FOUR
YEARS IN ROW AND WON 20 OR MORE GAMES
EIGHT SUCCESSIVE TIMES. LED LEAGUE IN
STRIKEOUTS FIVE YEARS AND LED OR TIED
FOR MOST SHUTOUTS FIVE TIMES.

ALBERT SPALDING

There is no telling how many records Albert Goodwill Spalding might have racked up if he had not given up his flourishing baseball career and focused his energies on his sporting goods business.

Spalding was but 17 years old when he pitched the Forest City team of Rockford, Illinois, to victory over the Washington National baseball club. That performance transformed Spalding into a national sports hero, serving as the first rung up in a career that would make his name synonymous with baseball as athlete and entrepreneur.

A superb pitcher, the first professional ever to win 200 games, Spalding led Boston to their four consecutive National Association titles. He posted a 56–4 record in 1875—the apex season of his time with Boston.

Then William Hulbert made him an offer he could not refuse: a $500 raise and the promise of a quarter of the White Stockings' gate. His stats there boggle the mind: 47 wins, 13 losses, a .783 percentage for the pennant-winning Chicago White Stockings of 1876.

Spalding quit when he at was truly at the top of his athletic form. Just after the start of the 1877 season, he gave up pitching to become a full-time promoter and businessman. Along with the Chicago White Stockings and another team comprised of National League and American Association all-stars, Spalding staged the 1888–1889 World Tour to bring baseball around the globe. The "baseball tourists" played ball in such destinations as Egypt, Australia, Italy, Britain, Hawaii, Ceylon, and Paris. In 1900, Spalding was appointed by President McKinley as the U.S. commissioner at that year's Summer Olympic Games.

Death came to Spalding on September 9, 1915, in Point Loma, California. Hall of Fame admission came in 1939. His plaque reads:

> ALBERT GOODWILL SPALDING
> ORGANIZATIONAL GENIUS OF BASEBALL'S
> PIONEER DAYS. STAR PITCHER OF FOREST
> CITY CLUB IN LATE 1860'S, 4-YEAR
> CHAMPION BOSTONS 1871–1875 AND
> MANAGER-PITCHER OF CHAMPION
> CHICAGOS IN NATIONAL LEAGUE'S FIRST
> YEAR. CHICAGO PRESIDENT FOR 10
> YEARS. ORGANIZER OF BASEBALL'S FIRST
> ROUND-THE-WORLD TOUR IN 1888.

BOBBY WALLACE

Roderick John Wallace, better known as Bobby Wallace, played in the major leagues for 25 years—six of those years the last ones of the 19th century. His great claim to fame was revolutionizing the way the position of shortstop was played.

Formerly a pitcher, an outfielder, a second baseman, and a third baseman, Wallace was shifted to shortstop in 1899 as a member of the St. Louis team.

"Right off, I knew I had found my dish," he recalled. Previously shortstops had fielded a ground ball, straightened up, and then thrown the ball. Wallace innovated a new style the scoop-and-toss.

"I noticed," he recalled, "more and more runners were beating out infield hoppers by a fraction of a second. It was apparent I had to learn to throw from the ankle and off balance as well." He learned well and in 1953 was the first American League shortstop to be elected to baseball's Hall of Fame. His plaque reads:

RODERICK J. WALLACE
CLEVELAND–ST. LOUIS–CINCINNATI N.L
ST. LOUIS A.L.—1894 TO 1918
ONE OF LONGEST CAREERS IN MAJOR
LEAGUES. OVER 60 YEARS AS PITCHER,
THIRD–BASEMAN, SHORTSTOP, MANAGER,
UMPIRE AND SCOUT. ACTIVE AS PLAYER
FOR 25 YEARS. SET A.L. RECORD FOR
CHANCES IN ONE GAME AT SHORTSTOP, 17,
JUNE 10, 1902. RECOGNIZED AS ONE OF
GREATEST SHORTSTOPS. PITCHED FOR
CLEVELAND IN 1896 TEMPLE CUP SERIES.

JOHN MONTGOMERY WARD

One of the true superstars of early baseball, John Montgomery Ward was one of the most versatile figures of his time. The handsome Ward, a graduate of Columbia University Law School, was one of those who laid the groundwork for the Brotherhood of Professional Base Ball Players, which gave rise to the Players League.

In his first major league start in July 1878, Ward, pitching for the Providence Grays, tossed a 3–0 shutout against the Indianapolis Hoosiers in his first major league start. From 1878 to 1882, Ward was a member of the Grays, shuttling between the pitching mound, the infield, and the outfield. He won 87 games in 1879–1880.

Ward was traded to the New York Giants in 1883, and although his days of pitching effectiveness were behind him, he had many years of winning baseball left. He taught himself how to switch-hit. And he taught himself how to steal bases, twice leading the league in that category. Ward even managed the Giants in the final 14 games of the 1884 season.

It was during his time with the Giants that he became one of the leaders in the Brotherhood—an odd role for one of the better-paid players of his time, a figure who was married to a beautiful actress, a man who was the toast of New York City society.

Ward was a manager again from 1890–1894, but retired from baseball at age 34 to concentrate solely on his legal practice, which involved baseball players. Later on, for a time he was part-owner of the Boston Braves and throughout the rest of his life kept involved with baseball in some capacity. He died in Augusta, Georgia, in 1925 and was admitted to the Hall of Fame in 1964. His plaque reads:

JOHN MONTGOMERY WARD
1878–1894
PITCHING PIONEER WHO WON 158,
LOST 102 GAMES IN SEVEN YEARS.
PITCHED PERFECT GAME FOR PROVIDENCE
OF N.L. IN 1880.
TURNED TO SHORTSTOP AND MADE 2,151 HITS.
MANAGED NEW YORK AND BROOKLYN IN N.L.
PRESIDENT OF BOSTON, N.L. 1911–1912.
PLAYED IMPORTANT PART IN ESTABLISHING
MODERN ORGANIZED BASEBALL.

GEORGE WRIGHT

The star player on the fabled Cincinnati Red Stockings and the brother of manager Harry Wright, George Wright was one of those who revolutionized the way the position of shortstop was played. Placing himself deep on the infield instead of on the base paths, as had previously been the style, Wright took advantage of his powerful arm to make the long throw to cut down a runner.

"George fielded hard-hit balls bare-handed," recalled his teammate Deacon White. "He gathered them up and speared them when in the air with either hand. He was an expert and accurate thrower, being able to throw with either hand."

From 1872 to 1875, George Wright teamed with his brother Harry to help Boston win four championships in the National Association. His last playing season was 1882, as a member of the Providence Grays, the team he had managed to the pennant in 1879. Thus, in the space of eight years, Wright starred on seven championship teams.

With a partner, Wright organized the Wright and Ditson sporting goods business in 1871. It was a business that went on to enjoy international success. In 1884, the Wright and Ditson baseball was used as the official ball by the Union Association. Hall of Fame acceptance came to Wright in 1937, the year of his death. His plaque reads:

GEORGE WRIGHT
STAR OF BASEBALL'S FIRST
PROFESSIONAL TEAM, THE
CINCINNATI RED STOCKINGS OF 1869.
GREAT SHORTSTOP AND CAPTAIN OF
CHAMPION BOSTONS IN NATIONAL
LEAGUE'S PIONEER YEARS.

HARRY WRIGHT

One of the most important figures in the long history of the national pastime, Harry Wright was known in some quarters as the "father of professional baseball."

The man who organized and led the fabled Cincinnati Red Stockings, Wright also inaugurated cooperative team play, hand signs for coaching, tours of foreign countries by baseball teams, and even knickers as part of a baseball uniform. He managed Boston to four straight pennants in the National Association—the first time this had ever been done by any team.

"Every magnate in the country is indebted to this man," the *Reach Guide* noted in 1896, a year after his death, "for the establishment of baseball as a business, and every patron for fulfilling him with a systematic recreation. Every player is indebted to him for inaugurating an occupation in which he gains a livelihood, and the country at large for adding one more industry . . . to furnish employment."

Harry Wright, born in Sheffield, England, the son of a professional cricket player, was admitted to baseball's Hall of Fame in 1953. His plaque reads:

HARRY WRIGHT

MANAGER AND CENTERFIELDER OF FAMOUS
CINCINNATI RED STOCKINGS, UNDEFEATED
IN 69 GAMES IN 1869–1870. FIRST MANAGER
TO WIN FOUR STRAIGHT PENNANTS WITH
BOSTON NATIONAL ASSOCIATION 1872–73–74
75. BROTHER OF GEORGE WRIGHT ALSO IN
HALL OF FAME. SPONSORED FIRST BASEBALL
TOUR TO ENGLAND IN 1876. INTRODUCED
KNICKER UNIFORMS. HIT 7 HOME RUNS IN
GAME AT NEWPORT, KY. IN 1867.

CY YOUNG

The statistics compiled by Cy Young in a fabled baseball career have earned him a reputation as one of the greatest pitchers of all time. For the decade of the 1890s, he averaged 27 wins and a 3.05 ERA. Young began his major league career in 1890 as a member of the Cleveland Spiders and finished it in 1911. And when he was done, he had won 511 games—more victories than any other pitcher in history.

Out of Gilmore, Ohio, Young was a husky right-hander. The former Ohio farm boy's formal name was Denton True Young, but his nickname "Cy," short for "Cyclone," was apt. "I thought I had to show all my stuff and I almost tore the boards off the grandstand with my fastball."

His fastball came up to the plate with blinding speed. Young posted 27 wins for Cleveland in his first full season and the following year won 36 games. In his 22-year career Young won 20 games a season 16 times, and five times won 30 games or more. He also recorded three no-hitters, including an 1897 perfect game over Cincinnati.

In the all-time rankings of pitchers, Young is first in wins (as well as losses), complete games, and innings pitched; fourth in career shutouts; and third in games appeared in. His pitching time moved way beyond the Gilded Age covering more than 22 seasons. One reason for his longevity was his ability to warm up by just throwing a few pitches and to be ready to pitch after just a day's rest. Durability was his trademark.

The 6' 2", 210-pound right-hander credited his off-season farm work, chopping wood and doing heavy chores, with keeping him in shape to play until he was 44 years old. By then he had seen it all.

Hall of Fame admission was in 1937. His plaque reads:

DENTON T. (CY) YOUNG

CLEVELAND (N) 1890–98

ST. LOUIS (N) 1899–1900

BOSTON (A) 1901–08

CLEVELAND (A) 1909–11

BOSTON (N) 1911

ONLY PITCHER IN FIRST HUNDRED

YEARS OF BASEBALL TO WIN 500 GAMES.

AMONG HIS 511 VICTORIES WERE 3

NO-HIT SHUTOUTS. PITCHED PERFECT

GAME MAY 5, 1904, NO OPPOSING

BATSMAN REACHING FIRST BASE.

SIX

The Great Teams

Oh, toot it somewhere else. Come to our ball park and see Anson pop
'em into Lake Michigan.
—fans of Chicago's baseball team

THE CHICAGO WHITE STOCKINGS

Winners of the first pennant in National League history, the
Chicago White Stockings won six pennants in the first 11 years of
the league's existence. The dominant team of the 1880s, the White
Stockings posted a winning percentage of .636 over 10 seasons. In
the years 1880–1890, Chicago's lowest finish was fourth place. The
White Stockings rolled to pennants in 1880, 1881, 1882, 1885, and
1886. They won 67 of 84 games, including 22 in a row, for a record
percentage of .798 in 1880.

Driven by player-manager Adrian "Cap" Anson, who was not
content for his team just to be the best in the National League,
Chicago became a baseball team always on the move: Anson wanted
his "Heroic Legion of Baseball" to be known as the best team any-
where. The White Stockings played exhibition games against all types
of opposition in all types of settings.

It was a gala event for the small towns that were visited by Anson
and his team. Sometimes Chicago players were outfitted in white
stockings and Dutch pants. One season they were resplendent,

dressed in white-bosomed shirts and dark dress suits. Traveling with a full entourage of helpers and hangers-on, the players arrived in the little hamlets of America seated in handsome open carriages drawn by white horses. And as the crowd assembled, Anson in that booming voice of his gave the curious onlookers his patented pitch.

Connie Mack, who would go on to a fabled baseball career as player, manager, and owner, recalled a visit by the Chicago team to his town of East Brookfield, Massachusetts, in 1883:

> We went over and looked over the sandlot where Anson's Chicago team was to play an exhibition game. It was a vacant lot littered with what I once called Irish confetti: tin cans, plug-tobacco tags. . . . Some of the others and I were working in the shoe factory, and we used our lunch hours to dump the debris . . . from what we called the diamond. We wanted to get it out of our sight so that our Chicago visitors wouldn't stumble over it.
>
> . . . The gala day in East Brookfield found all the villagers trying to see the game. It was a bigger event to us than the inauguration of a president. We cheered ourselves hoarse as Anson and [his team] trotted onto our sandlot. What a glorious sight it was. Anson played first base. A little fellow named Nichol played in right field. What a roar he got from us East Brookfielders when he ran up behind the great Anson and sneaked between his legs! Cap, who was a born showman, appeared to be surprised and bewildered. We nearly burst our buttons with laughter at the spectacle.
>
> When it was over, we passed the hat to raise the $100 guarantee for our visitors. Dimes, nickels, and pennies fell into it. When we counted these we found we had just enough. With a rousing ovation from old East Brookfield, we waved our hats good-bye as Anson and his galloping Colts left our hometown.

Not all the Chicago games took place before overflow crowds. On September 27, 1881, the White Stockings of Chicago played against Troy, New York. The contest was meaningless—the Chicago team had locked up the pennant and Troy had a lock on mediocrity. The weather was miserable; it rained and rained. The only thing that made the contest memorable was the 12 fans in attendance: that wet dozen ranks as the smallest paid attendance in major league baseball history.

The innovator of spring training, the first pilot to coordinate infield and outfield play, the first manager to coach from the baselines and institute a pitching rotation, Cap Anson, at 6 feet, 2 inches tall and more than 200 pounds, was a giant for those days. His creed echoed his feeling for power: "Round up the strongest men who can knock a baseball the farthest the most often, put yourself on first base, and win."

The Chicago infield was known in the mid-1880s as the "Stone Wall." Baseball's first superstar, player-manager Anson held down first base. Ned Williamson, "the greatest all-around player the country ever saw," in Anson's phrase, was at third base; in a decade plus a year with Chicago, he batted .259, including 27 home runs in 1884, when what had formerly been ground-rule doubles at Lake Front Stadium were counted as homers. Tommy Burns was the shortstop; second base was manned by Fred Pfeffer.

The outfield from 1880 to 1886 consisted of George Gore in center, Abner Dalrymple in left, and the illustrious Mike "King" Kelly in right field. Twice the flamboyant Kelly led the National League in batting and three times in runs scored.

Anson characterized Kelly as "as great a hitter as anyone and as great a thrower, both from the catcher's position and the field, more men being thrown out by him than any other man." However, it was the exuberant Kelly's base-stealing dramatics that earned him his storied reputation. Kelly's version of the hook slide was encouraged by Anson and immortalized in the song "Slide, Kelly, Slide." The tune was sung with verve whenever Kelly reached base. And Kelly would launch himself head first, feet spread, toward second base, dramatically completing his run and slide with the tactic known as the "Kelly spread."

William A. "Billy" Sunday was the team's utility outfielder from 1884 to 1887. Anson allegedly discovered Sunday in a race in Marshalltown, Iowa. In Anson's view, Sunday, who would go on to become a world-famed evangelist, "ran like a deer" and was the fastest man in baseball.

Frank "Old Silver" Flint handled the pitching staff. The catcher's mask troubled him ("I can't breathe with the damned thing").

Chicago pitchers included John Clarkson, who was admitted to the Baseball Hall of Fame in 1963. In 1885, his second year with the White Stockings, the Massachusetts native won 53 games, including a no-hitter against Providence. In three full campaigns with Chicago, Clarkson averaged 268 strikeouts a season and compiled a won-lost record of 137–57.

Other star hurlers for "Anson's Athletes" included slowball pitcher Fred "Goldy" Goldsmith, winner of 98 games in his four full seasons with the Pale Hose; and Brooklyn-born Larry Corcoran, a hard throwing right-hander who posted three no-hitters and a 190–83 record over five seasons with Chicago.

The Chicago team of 1882 was rated the best by King Kelly. "There were seven of us, six feet high," he recalled. "Fred Pfeffer, the second baseman, could lay on his stomach and throw a ball a hundred yards. We wore silk stockings and the best uniforms money could buy. We had 'em whipped before we even threw a ball. We had 'em scared ter death." That 1882 team destroyed Cleveland, 35–4, on July 24. Dalrymple, Kelly, Gore, Williamson, Burns, Flint, and Hugh Nichol each managed four hits to set a major league record.

"Inside baseball"—coordination of infield and outfield play, cautious base running, and a scientific, though by today's standards basic, approach—marked the managing techniques of Anson and became a standard that others emulated.

On the playing field, he tormented umpires. "That ain't no shadow," a fan observed as the huge manager's 220-pound figure was outlined by the sun on the diamond. "That's an argument. Everywhere Cap goes there's an argument."

In 1890, the Chicago team managed perhaps its finest moment. Racked by player desertions to the Brotherhood League, Anson's roster was depleted of virtually all its regulars. Anson patched together a team he picked up from the minors, from sandlots, from town teams. Fans called them Anson's Colts. Old Pop Anson batted .342 that year and marched Chicago to a second-place finish just five games behind Brooklyn—a team that had sustained no losses to the renegade Brotherhood League.

Anson was 40 years old in 1891 and was hitting slightly below .300. Writers suggested he might be better off if he retired. On September 4, the proud Anson played an entire game sporting fake whiskers in a not-so-covert mockery of his detractors.

The later decline of Anson as a player and various injuries to key Chicago stars finally brought White Stocking domination of the National League to an end. In 1897, Anson, playing in his final season, became the oldest player ever to hit .300. And on July 18 of that year he became the first major leaguer to collect 3,000 hits. The following season, Anson was replaced as player-manager and an era ended. Chicago's new nickname was the Orphans—a tag that stayed with them through the rest of the 19th century.

THE PROVIDENCE GRAYS

A pennant winner in 1879 and 1884, the Providence (Rhode Island) Grays wound up in second place in the years in between and furnished spirited competition for the Chicago White Stockings. Managed by Harry Wright, the Grays boasted players who became baseball legends: John Montgomery Ward, George Wright, and Charles "Old Hoss" Radbourn. They played their home games at Messer Street Grounds in the Olneyville neighborhood, as one of the eight teams in the National League.

Ward won 84 games for Providence in 1879–1880, including a perfect game against Buffalo. Radbourn was a one-man army in 1884, pitching Providence to the pennant, starting and finishing 73 of the Grays' 112 games, and recording a 60–12 mark. His 441 strikeouts and almost 630 innings pitched led the league in those categories. That year, the Providence Grays won 84 games and lost 28.

The spirited 1882 pennant competition between the White Stockings and Grays excited the world of 19th-century baseball and epitomized the rivalry between the two teams. Chicago trailed Providence by five games in late June, and its chances of repeating as pennant winners against a strong Providence team were considered slim; however, the Stockings swept the Grays in Chicago in mid-September before overflow crowds that milled about in the outfield grass as Corcoran and Goldsmith outpitched Ward and Radbourn. The sweep enabled Chicago to move on to win the pennant by three games.

In a curious footnote to the baseball history of the team, it may have been the first in the majors to have an African-American baseball player: William Edward White, a Brown University player who played one game for the Grays on June 21, 1879. Strong but inconclusive evidence exists as researched by Peter Morris of the Society for American Baseball Research.

The Providence Grays disbanded after the 1885 season.

THE NEW YORK GIANTS

Boasting a lineup that contained a half-dozen future Hall of Famers, the New York Giants won the National League pennant in 1888 and waged a furious fight for the flag against Chicago in 1885 and 1886. The nickname of the team originated in the 1880s when manager Jim Mutrie, commenting on the large size of his players and urging them on to victory during the course of a close game, bellowed: "My big fellows! My giants! We are the people!"

Mutrie's men included John Montgomery Ward, who came to the Giants from Providence in 1883; fiery William "Buck" Ewing, an Ohioan who recorded a better-than-.300 average in each of his seven seasons with the New Yorkers and earned $5,000 a year during the 1890s, the top salary of the time; and James "Orator Jim" O'Rourke, an outfielder and sometimes infielder, sometimes catcher, who batted over .300 eight times in 19 seasons. And although overshadowed by Cap Anson, Giant first baseman Roger Connor was a genuine star in his own right; the following season, Connor notched a league-record 17 home runs.

Right-hander Tim "Sir Timothy" Keefe, the premier hurler on the team, was 169–76 during his half-decade with the Giants from

1885 to 1889. Keefe designed the uniform of the Giants—an all-black outfit with white lettering.

Michael "Smiling Mickey" Welch, a 6-foot, 3-inch, 190-pound southpaw, took turns as a starter for the New Yorkers along with Keefe. In 1885 Welch recorded 44 triumphs and a league-leading .800 winning percentage. Welch attributed the reason for his pitching success to his consumption of beer. "Pure elixir of malt and hops," he bragged. "Beats all the drugs and all the drops."

The Giants, with Welch and Keefe combining for 66 victories, battled the White Stockings for the National League pennant in 1885 down to the final days of the season. In a four-game series in Chicago before standing-room-only throngs of more than 10,000, the White Stockings won three of the four games.

The not-too-objective *Chicago Tribune*, comparing the differences between the two teams, observed that the crucial element was not speed nor brawn but "strategy. . . . The White Stockings play a more brainy game."

The Gay Nineties saw a turn in the fortunes of the Giants as managers came and went. The saber-mustached Mutrie retired in 1891, and 13 other pilots took a shot at directing the fortunes of the team. All these efforts were to no avail until John J. McGraw arrived on the scene in 1902 and brought back the glory days of the team.

THE ST. LOUIS BROWNS

The American Association Browns of St. Louis, owned by beer baron Chris Von der Ahe, managed four straight pennants in 1885–1888 and second-place finishes in 1883 and 1889. Stars on the Browns included player-manager Charles Comiskey, Arlie Latham, Dave Foutz, and Bob Caruthers. To acquire Caruthers, Von der Ahe purchased the entire Minneapolis franchise, while the fee for Foutz was the entire Bay City franchise.

Nicknames for the St. Louis players were not too complimentary, but they were apt. Third baseman Latham richly deserved the label "the Freshest Man on the Earth." At one point he had 20 post-season brawls scheduled—and five of those fistic encounters were slated against his own teammates. Pitcher Caruthers, the "Mighty Mite," was aptly tagged but seldom tagged by batters. Caruthers posted a 218–99 record for nine years through 1892, placing him first in winning percentage among all those hurlers who ever performed in the major leagues.

Charlie Comiskey, the player-manager, built his team on solid base running, strong fielding, and brilliant pitching. The man they would call the "Old Roman" also viewed heckling the opposition as part of his team's game plan. "About the toughest and roughest gang that ever struck this city is the nine of the St. Louis Club. Vile of speech, insolent in bearing . . . they set at defiance all rules, grossly insulting the umpire and exciting the wrath of the spectators." Oddly enough, that less than complimentary characterization was the observation of a St. Louis writer. Out-of-town journalists expressed earthier sentiments.

In 1892, after the American Association folded as a major league, the Browns returned to the National League. In the next seven years, Von der Ahe's men wound up 12th in a 12-team league twice and managed a fifth-place finish just once. Selling off stars and firing managers at a furious pace, "Der Poss Bresident" destroyed his entire winning and money-making operation. After the 1898 season, the other National League owners had seen enough, and they forced Von der Ahe to sell out for the meager sum of $35,000. It is rumored that he muttered all that time: "Too late schmart."

THE BALTIMORE ORIOLES

The greatest team of its era was the 1890s Baltimore Orioles. Almost a third of the major league players in the 1890s were Irish—a reflection of the immigrant waves that were swelling America. And the Orioles, too, were possessed of an Irish flavor: manager Ned Hanlon, John J. McGraw, Hughie Jennings, Wee Willie Keeler, Jack Doyle, Joe Kelley, among others.

The Orioles won pennants in the 12-team National League in 1894, 1895, and 1896 and batted .332 as a team during that span of time. They finished in second place in 1897 and 1898.

"Oriole baseball" was tough baseball, innovative baseball, baseball of the next century: the hit-and-run, the backing up of throws, the positioning of players to take outfield relays. Baseballs hidden in the outfield grass miraculously appeared on cue in the glove of a Baltimore outfielder and an amazed batter would be held to a single, rarely more than that. On the base paths, wide hips and clenched fists characterized the spirit of the Orioles.

The lively Oriole team frequently started its practices at 8 A.M., and that was in an era when games began late in the afternoon. The time was well used, as the Orioles refined their skills and readied their tricks.

Manager Ned Hanlon diligently drilled all his Orioles in the fine art of bunting to capitalize on the rules change that had moved the pitcher's mound from 50 feet to 60 feet, 6 inches from the plate. And Hanlon instructed his groundskeeper to keep the grass growing high near the foul lines to help keep bunts in fair territory. The infield was also given special treatment. Kept rock-hard, that surface became the launching pad for the "Baltimore chop"—O's hitters smashed down hard on the ball, pounding it into the cement-hard infield, and scampered to first base before infielders could gather up the ball.

Fake throws, feigned steals, actual steals (six of the Baltimore regulars had 30 or more in 1894), superbly executed cutoff plays—all of these had the Oriole opposition reeling. "This isn't baseball they're playing," moaned Giants manager Monte Ward in 1894. "It's an entirely different game. I'm going to bring them up before league president Young."

A devil-may-care attitude and a legendary toughness were part of the Oriole way. Running down a long drive to the outfield fence, mashing his arm through the barbed wire, Willie Keeler still managed to make the catch and save a game against Washington even though he ripped his arm all the way up to his elbow.

The Orioles became known for "inside baseball." The tactic as applied to fielding was miraculous. When a ball was hit by an opposing batter, all the O's would shift gears and move about to new positions, depending on where the ball was hit. For example, if the ball was smacked to left field, the third baseman would race onto the outfield grass, positioned for a relay throw. Third base would be covered by the shortstop. The second baseman covered his own position. Backup coverage was provided by the catcher and pitcher for overthrows, while the center fielder also got into the act by moving closer to the left fielder in case of difficulty. The 1892 Orioles had committed 584 errors and posted the worst fielding average in the National League. The 1893 team with the new fielding approach at work reduced its errors to 293. And Baltimore leaped from a last-place finish in 1892 to a first-place finish in 1893. Oriole success was the final nail in the coffin of the 500-error season.

The 1894 Oriole season batting averages reveal just how powerful an attack the team was able to mount: McGraw, .340; Keller, .371; Kelley, .393; Brouthers, .347; Jennings, .332; Brodie, .369; Reitz, .309; and Robinson, .348. The Baltimore powerhouse won 24 of its last 25 games. "We would have won all twenty-five," bellowed John J. McGraw, "if Robbie [Wilbert Robinson, the catcher] hadn't slipped going after a foul fly. The clumsy ox."

Robinson, the team captain, always claimed, "I was the soft soap artist of that crew. The umpires would call a close one against us, and somebody, usually McGraw, would come storming in." That would lead to violent protesting until Robinson would intervene and attempt to placate the umpire to prevent having McGraw or other irate Orioles ejected.

"Robinson was the sugar," cracked McGraw, "and I was the vinegar." Only once in his entire Baltimore career was Robinson tossed out of a game. After that, he devoted his energies to maintaining his handlebar mustache and maximizing his baseball talent, which was as considerable as his growing girth.

One of the legendary stars of the Orioles was William Henry Keeler, but his short stature (5 feet, 4 inches) and slight weight (140 pounds) earned him the nickname "Wee Willie." Keeler's bat was also undernourished, weighing just 30 ounces. Keeler's greatest year was 1897, when he batted .432, recorded 243 hits, stole 64 bases, and scored 145 runs. In 1898 the left-handed bat magician collected 202 singles in 128 games—the most singles in a season by anyone who has ever played the game.

The most truculent of the Orioles was John J. "Mugsy" McGraw. Slapping the ball out of an infielder's glove, brandishing his well-sharpened spikes, switching baseballs in mid-play, berating and belittling umpires, opponents, and opposing fans—all of these were part of McGraw's tricks of his trade.

One of the stars who was lost in the galaxy on the Orioles was Hughie Jennings. Acquired by Baltimore in 1893, Jennings was hobbled by a sore arm and played very little, managing to get into only 16 games. He sat on the bench and learned "inside baseball" from manager Ned Hanlon. And whenever he could, he nursed his arm in the warmth of a brick kiln. It must have helped, for from 1895 to 1897, Jennings batted .386, .398, and .355.

"Jennings, Kelley, Keeler, Robinson, and myself," McGraw mused, "organized ourselves into a sort of committee. We were scheming all the time for a new kind of stunt to pull. We met every night and talked over our successes and failures. We talked, lived, dreamed baseball."

THE BOSTON BEANEATERS

Up until 1887, the Boston National League team was known as the Red Stockings or Reds, but the Cincinnati team was the one most identified with that nickname. In 1887 the Hub club became known as the Beaneaters.

In the last quarter of the 19th century, Boston finished on top of the National League eight times; however, the New Englanders really got it going in the 1890s—winning the pennant in 1891, 1892, 1893, 1897, and 1898.

The ace of the pitching staff during those glorious years in Boston was Charles "Kid" Nichols. During each of the pennant-winning seasons, the Kid won 29 or more games. Lacking a curveball, he utilized speed and control, working his trade off a smooth overhand delivery. Nichols seemed always to have Baltimore's number. "You always know what the Kid is going to throw," complained Oriole manager Ned Hanlon, "but he beats you anyway."

Hugh Duffy supplied much of the punch for Boston. In 1888 Duffy had been a member of the White Stockings, but Cap Anson was not enamored of him. "Hughie," Anson said, "you fall about five inches and twenty-five pounds short of major league size. The boys will eat you alive."

Duffy led the league in hits, doubles, home runs, runs batted in, and slugging percentage. Duffy and his outfield buddy Tom McCarthy formed the Boston tandem that was known as the "Heavenly Twins." McCarthy earned a footnote in baseball history by prompting the rule change that governed when a player could leave a base after a fly ball was hit. McCarthy would allow the ball to hit in his glove and then juggle the ball as he raced into the infield. Only when he realized that it was impossible for a runner to advance would he cease and desist his juggling act and take full possession of the ball.

The Boston double-play combo for most of their winning years was Bobby Lowe and Herman "Germany" Long. Lowe lowered the boom on opposing pitchers one sunny afternoon at the Boston Congress Street Grounds in 1894. He bashed two third-inning home runs. Then he homered again in the fifth inning. Then he homered again in the sixth inning. The hometown crowd was agog—it was the first time in major league history that a player had homered four times in one game. The game was stopped and the jumping and jubilant fans rewarded Lowe with $160 worth of silver. In the eighth inning, all Lowe could muster was a single. And it is rumored that some of the disappointed fans wanted their money back.

The most disappointing season during the Gay Nineties for Boston fans was 1894, a year the Beaneaters attempted to win their fourth straight pennant. Duffy batted .438, seven players scored more than a hundred runs, and not once was the team shut out. Yet, when it was all over, Boston, who trailed Baltimore by just a half game heading into the final month of the season, faded and had to settle for a third-place finish.

One of the major reasons for the success of the Boston team was the braininess of its manager, taciturn Frank Selee, a tremendous judge of baseball talent—like Fred Tenney and Jimmie Collins. Both became fixtures at the corners for the last two Boston championship teams of the 19th century, in 1897 and 1898. First baseman Tenney came right off the campus of Brown University, while Collins was a graduate of the Buffalo, New York, sandlots. For seven straight seasons, Tenney batted over .300. He originated the 3–6–3 double play and played wide and deep, foreshadowing the positioning of modern-day first basemen. Collins, innovator of the quick pickup and throw of slowly hit balls, is rated as one of the greatest third basemen of all time.

Poised for the 20th century, Boston was a city and a team proud of its past—five pennants in eight years and eight pennants since the formation of the National League in 1876.

Epilogue

Verily, the National game is Great!
—Sporting Life

Despite the naysayers that have surfaced through the decades, baseball is still our national pastime. And the long legacy of those who played the game bare-handed on rutted fields in darkening daylight is still also a part of the game.

Baseball is still comforting regularity, a sport played and viewed from childhood on. It is still the individual battle of pitcher against batter, the movements of the fielders, adjusting, the signs relayed, received. Baseball is still shading, nuance, degree, foreshadowing, interval, climax.

Its tempo is still 19th century—prescribed by the game and not by the clock.

The season extends from the early green days of spring through the steam of summery nights and the blaze of August afternoons, into the bittersweet chill of the 10th month of the year, October—and sometimes even November.

Half the time the games of a team are played at home; half the time the games of a team are played on the road.

And there is time enough for rivalries to be renewed, for heroes to emerge.

The timeless ritual of the set lineup, the fixed positions, echoes back to baseball's beginnings. Four men in the infield, three men in the outfield, the pitcher throwing the ball on a white line to the plate, to the batter, to the catcher.

Baseball is the record of the program, the scorecard, the yearbook, the line score. Baseball is the sound of the crack of the wood of the bat against the ball, the smack of the ball against the leather of the glove, the roar of the crowd, the rule of the umpire, the noise of the players.

Baseball is an evocation of another time, another century.

The geometry of the diamond and the pastureland of the outfield play back the simple feel of an orderly, agrarian America.

Split-screen images intertwine: Wee Willie Keeler and Pete Rose, John J. McGraw and Tony LaRussa, Cy Young and Nolan Ryan, Billy Hamilton and Lou Brock, Buck Ewing and Johnny Bench, Dan Brouthers and Albert Pujols.

The story of the game links the centuries, joins the generations. Baseball's past is as real as its present, always close to the surface, always worth celebrating.

APPENDIXES

For the Record

Anybody with a pencil could be a statistician back then
[in the 19th century].
Seymour Siwoff, Elias Sports Bureau

APPENDIX A

NATIONAL LEAGUE PENNANT WINNERS

Year	Club	Manager	Won	Lost	Pct.
1876	Chicago	Albert G. Spalding	52	14	.788
1877	Boston	Harry Wright	31	17	.646
1878	Boston	Harry Wright	41	19	.683
1879	Providence	George Wright	55	23	.705
1880	Chicago	Adrian C. Anson	67	17	.798
1881	Chicago	Adrian C. Anson	56	28	.667
1882	Chicago	Adrian C. Anson	55	29	.655
1883	Boston	John F. Morrill	63	35	.643
1884	Providence	Frank C. Bancroft	84	28	.750
1885	Chicago	Adrian C. Anson	87	25	.777
1886	Chicago	Adrian C. Anson	90	34	.726
1887	Detroit	William H. Watkins	79	45	.637
1888	New York	James Mutrie	84	47	.641
1889	New York	James Mutrie	83	43	.659

Year	Club	Manager	Won	Lost	Pct.
1890	Brooklyn	William McGunnigle	86	43	.667
1891	Boston	Frank Selee	87	51	.630
1892	Boston	Frank Selee	102	48	.680
1893	Boston	Frank Selee	86	44	.662
1894	Baltimore	Edward H. Hanlon	89	39	.695
1895	Baltimore	Edward H. Hanlon	87	43	.669
1896	Baltimore	Edward H. Hanlon	90	39	.698
1897	Boston	Frank Selee	93	39	.705
1898	Boston	Frank Selee	102	47	.685
1899	Brooklyn	Edward H. Hanlon	88	42	.677
1900	Brooklyn	Edward H. Hanlon	82	54	.603

APPENDIX B

NATIONAL LEAGUE
HOME RUN CHAMPIONS

Year	Club	Player	Home Runs
1876	Philadelphia	George Hall	5
1877	Louisville	George Shaffer	3
1878	Providence	Paul A. Hines	4
1879	Boston	Charles W. Jones	9
1880	Boston	James H. O'Rourke	6
	Worcester	Harry D. Stovey	6
1881	Buffalo	Dennis Brouthers	8
1882	Detroit	George A. Wood	7
1883	New York	William Ewing	10
1884	Chicago	Edward N. Williamson	27
1885	Chicago	Abner F. Dalrymple	11
1886	Detroit	Arthur H. Richardson	11
1887	New York	Roger Connor	17
	Washington	William S. O'Brien	17
1888	New York	Roger Connor	14
1889	Philadelphia	Samuel L. Thompson	20
1890	Brooklyn	Thomas P. Burns	13
	New York	Michael J. Tiernan	13
1891	Boston	Harry D. Stovey	16
	New York	Michael J. Tiernan	16
1892	Cincinnati	James W. Holliday	13
1893	Philadelphia	Edward J. Delahanty	19
1894	Boston	Hugh Duffy	18
	Boston	Robert L. Lowe	18
1895	Washington	William M. Joyce	17
1896	Philadelphia	Edward J. Delahanty	13
	Philadelphia	Samuel L. Thompson	13
1897	Philadelphia	Napoleon Lajoie	10
1898	Boston	James J. Collins	14
1899	Washington	John F. Freeman	25
1900	Boston	Herman C. Long	12

APPENDIX C

NATIONAL LEAGUE BATTING CHAMPIONS

Year	Club	Player	Games	Hits	Avg.
1876	Chicago	Roscoe C. Barnes	66	138	.404
1877	Boston	James L. White	48	82	.385
1878	Milwaukee	Abner F. Dalrymple	60	95	.356
1879	Chicago	Adrian C. Anson	49	90	.407
1880	Chicago	George F. Gore	75	114	.365
1881	Chicago	Adrian C. Anson	84	217	.399
1882	Buffalo	Dennis Brouthers	84	129	.367
1883	Buffalo	Dennis Brouthers	97	156	.371
1884	Buffalo	James H. O'Rourke	104	157	.350
1885	New York	Roger Connor	110	169	.371
1886	Chicago	Michael J. Kelly	118	175	.388
1887	Chicago	Adrian C. Anson	122	224	.421
1888	Chicago	Adrian C. Anson	134	177	.343
1889	Boston	Dennis Brouthers	126	181	.373
1890	New York	John W. Glasscock	124	172	.336
1891	Philadelphia	William R. Hamilton	133	179	.338
1892	Brooklyn	Dennis Brouthers	152	197	.335
1893	Boston	Hugh Duffy	131	203	.378
1894	Boston	Hugh Duffy	124	236	.438
1895	Cleveland	Jesse C. Burkett	132	235	.423
1896	Cleveland	Jesse C. Burkett	133	240	.410
1897	Baltimore	William H. Keeler	128	243	.432
1898	Baltimore	William H. Keeler	128	214	.379
1899	Philadelphia	Edward J. Delahanty	145	234	.408
1900	Pittsburgh	John P. Wagner	134	201	.381

APPENDIX D

NATIONAL LEAGUE
BASE-STEALING CHAMPIONS

Year	Club	Player	Bases Stolen
1886	Philadelphia	George Andrews	56
1887	New York	John M. Ward	111
1888	Washington	William Hoy	82
1889	Philadelphia	James Fogarty	99
1890	Philadelphia	Billy Hamilton	102
1891	Philadelphia	Billy Hamilton	115
1892	Brooklyn	John M. Ward	94
1893	New York	John M. Ward	72
1894	Philadelphia	Billy Hamilton	99
1895	Philadelphia	Billy Hamilton	95
1896	Chicago	Bill Lange	100
1897	Chicago	Bill Lange	83
1898	Louisville	Fred Clarke	66
1899	Baltimore	Jimmy Sheckard	76
1900	Cincinnati	James Barrett	46

APPENDIX E

NATIONAL LEAGUE PITCHING LEADERS

Year	Club	Manager	Won	Lost	Pct.
1876	Chicago	A. G. Spalding	47	14	.770
1877	Boston	Thomas Bond	31	17	.646
1878	Boston	Thomas Bond	40	19	.678
1879	Providence	John M. Ward	44	18	.710
1880	Chicago	Fred Goldsmith	22	3	.880
1881	Chicago	Larry Corcoran	31	14	.689
1882	Chicago	Larry Corcoran	27	13	.675
1883	Cleveland	Jim McCormick	27	13	.675
1884	Providence	Charles Radbourn	60	12	.833
1885	Chicago	John Clarkson	53	16	.768
1886	Chicago	John Flynn	24	6	.800
1887	Detroit	Charles Getzein	29	13	.690
1888	New York	Tim Keefe	35	12	.745
1889	Boston	John Clarkson	48	19	.716
1890	Brooklyn	Tom Lovett	32	11	.744
1891	New York	John Ewing	22	8	.733
1892	Cleveland	Cy Young	36	10	.783
1893	Pittsburgh–Boston	Henry Gastright	15	6	.714
1894	New York	Jouett Meekin	35	11	.761
1895	Baltimore	Willie Hoffer	31	7	.816
1896	Baltimore	Willie Hoffer	26	7	.788
1897	New York	Amos Rusie	28	8	.778
1898	Boston	Ed Lewis	25	8	.758
1899	Brooklyn	Jay Hughes	25	5	.833
1900	Brooklyn	Joe McGinnity	20	6	.769

APPENDIX F

1890s LEADERS

Batting Average

Willie Keeler	.384
Billy Hamilton	.357
Jesse Burkett	.356
Ed Delahanty	.354
Joe Kelley	.340
Jake Stenzel	.339
Sam Thompson	.338
John McGraw	.336
Fred Clarke	.334
Hugh Duffy	.332

Home Runs

Hugh Duffy	83
Ed Delahanty	79
Mike Tiernan	77
Sam Thompson	75
Roger Connor	72

Hits

Ed Delahanty	1,862
Hugh Duffy	1,860
Jesse Burkett	1,798
George VanHaltren	1,782
Billy Hamilton	1,690

APPENDIX G

NATIONAL ASSOCIATION OF BASE BALL PLAYERS CHAMPIONS

Year	NABBP Champion	Best Record
1857	N/A	Brooklyn Atlantics (7–1–1)
1858	N/A	New York Mutuals (11–1)
		Brooklyn Atlantics (7–0)
1859	Brooklyn Atlantics (11–1)	Brooklyn Atlantics (11–1)
1860	Brooklyn Atlantics (12–2–2)[a]	Brooklyn Excelsiors (18–2–1)
1861	Brooklyn Atlantics (5–2)	New York Mutuals (8–2)
1862	Brooklyn Eckfords (14–2)	Brooklyn Eckfords (14–2)
1863	Brooklyn Eckfords (10–0)	Brooklyn Eckfords (10–0)
1864	Brooklyn Atlantics (20–0–1)	Brooklyn Atlantics (20–0–1)
1865	Brooklyn Atlantics (18–0)	Brooklyn Atlantics (18–0)
1866	Brooklyn Atlantics (17–3)	Unions of Morrisania (25–3)
		Philadelphia Athletics (23–2)
1867	Unions of Morrisania (21–8)	Philadelphia Athletics (44–3)
1868	New York Mutuals (31–10)	Philadelphia Athletics (47–3)
1869	Brooklyn Atlantics (40–6–2/15–6–1)	Cincinnati Red Stockings (57–0/19–0)
1870	Chicago White Stockings (65–8/22–7)[b]	Cincinnati Red Stockings (67–6–1/27–6–1)

Note: A new team could only win the National Association of Base Ball Players championship by defeating the reigning champion in a best-of-three-game series. With uneven scheduling, recording the most wins or even the highest winning percentage was not necessarily an accurate estimate of the best team. A team in a given year did not have the opportunity to play for the championship. For example, in 1868 and 1869, the undefeated 1869 Cincinnati Red Stockings swept their series with the 1868 champion Mutuals, but only after the Atlantics had done the same. Won–Lost records for 1869 and 1870 are shown separately for all games.

[a] The 1860 championship was officially retained by the Atlantics. In the decisive game, the Excelsiors were leading with men on base, but were forced to withdraw by a rowdy crowd. The game was declared a draw, and the championship was retained by the Atlantics.

[b] The 1870 championship was disputed by New York Mutuals. New York was leading 13–12 in the final game of their series when they vacated the field in protest. Officials decided to revert the score to the end of the last completed inning. The victory and championship were given to Chicago. The Mutuals, however, declared themselves champions for the year.

APPENDIX H

HOME RUN RECORD EVOLUTION

Year	Games	Player	Team	League	Home runs
1871	29	Lipman Pike	Troy Unions	NA	4
1871	28	Fred Treacey	Chicago NA	4	
1871	28	Levi Meyerle	Philadelphia Athletics	NA	4
1872	58	Lip Pike	Baltimore Canaries	NA	6
1875	82	Jim O'Rourke	Boston Red Stockings	NA	6
1879	84	Charley Jones	Boston Red Stockings	NL	9
1883	98	Harry Stovey	Philadelphia Athletics	AA	14
1884	112	Ned Williamson	Chicago White Stockings	NL	27[a]
1884	112	Dan Brouthers	Buffalo Blues	NL	14
1887	132	Billy O'Brien	Washington Nationals	NL	19
1889	132	Sam Thompson	Philadelphia Phillies	NL	20
1899	154	Buck Freeman	Washington Nationals	NL	25

Note: NA: National Association of Base Ball Players; NL: National League; AA: American Association.

[a] The 1884 27-home-run total of Ned Williamson is suspect. The left and right field fences in his home park were less than 250 feet from home plate. In past and future seasons, balls hit over these fences were ruled ground-rule doubles.

About the Author

Harvey Frommer is the celebrated author of 37 sports books, including the classics *New York City Baseball*, *Shoeless Joe and Ragtime Baseball*, *Rickey and Robinson*, *The New York Yankee Encyclopedia*, *A Yankee Century*, and the best-selling *Red Sox Vs. Yankees: The Great Rivalry* (with Frederic J. Frommer). Professor emeritus of the City University of New York and professor at Dartmouth College, where he teaches oral history and sports journalism, Frommer has been cited in the *Congressional Record* and honored by the New York State Legislature as a sports historian.